943.8
Gre

DISCARDED

DATE DUE

6552

Metro Litho
Oak Forest, IL 60452

02783-2

943.8 Greene, Carol
GRE   Poland

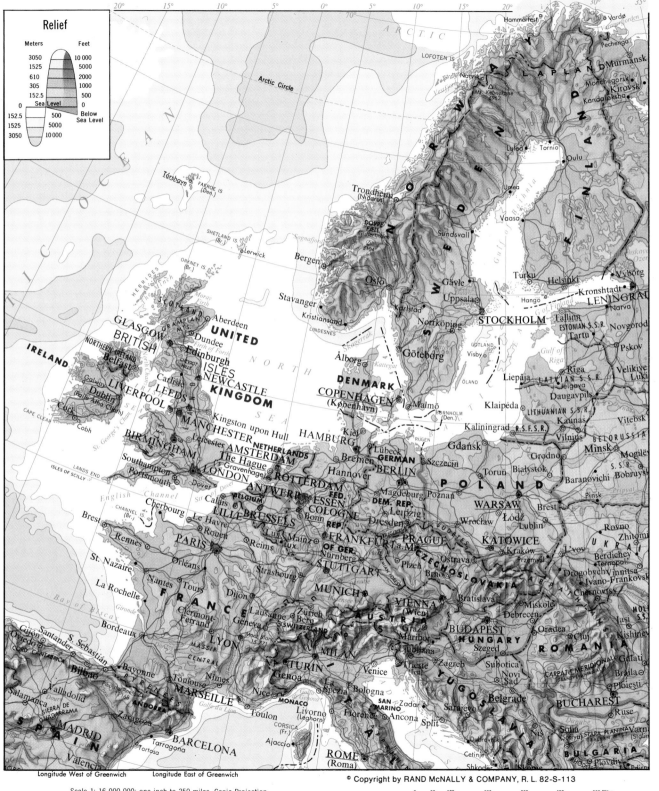

Relief

Meters	Feet
3050	10 000
1525	5000
610	2000
305	1000
152.5	500
0 Sea Level	0
152.5	500 Below
1525	5000 Sea Level
3050	10 000

Longitude West of Greenwich   Longitude East of Greenwich

© Copyright by RAND McNALLY & COMPANY, R. L. 82-S-113

Scale 1: 16 000 000; one inch to 250 miles. Conic Projection

Elevations and depressions are given in feet

| 0 | 50 | 100 | 200 | 300 | 400 | 500 Miles |

| 0 | 100 | 200 | 400 | 600 | 800 Kilometers |

Enchantment of the World

POLAND

by Carol Greene

Consultants: Thaddeus V. Gromada, Ph. D., Professor of History and Coordinator of Ethnic Studies at Jersey City State College and Secretary-General of the Polish Institute of Arts and Sciences in America and Anna M. Rychlinski, M.A., Polish Literature, City Desk Editor, *Polish Daily Zgoda*, Chicago, Illinois

Consultant for Social Studies: Donald W. Nylin, Ph. D., Assistant Superintendent for Instruction, Aurora West Public Schools, Aurora, Illinois

Consultant for Reading: Robert L. Hillerich, Ph. D., Bowling Green State University, Bowling Green, Ohio

CHILDRENS PRESS ™

CHICAGO

A lady from the country sells wild flowers (left) and a young girl eats a hot dog (opposite page) in Warsaw.

For Michael, Lucy, and Emily Kyle

Library of Congress Cataloging in Publication Data

Greene, Carol.
  Poland.

  (Enchantment of the world)
  Includes index.
  Summary: Describes the history, geography, industry, culture, and other features of this European country on the Baltic Sea.
  1. Poland—Juvenile literature. [1. Poland]
I. Title.
DK4040.G7 1983   943.8   82-19737
ISBN 0-516-02783-2   AACR2

Picture Acknowledgments
A-Stock Photo Finder—© David J. Maenza: pages 4, 21, 54, 89 (right)
Hillstrom Stock Photos—© Milt and Joan Mann: Cover, pages 5, 9, 13, 14, 16, 17, 18, 24, 25, 26, 58 (bottom), 59 (top), 60 (2 photos), 62 (bottom), 68, 71, 72, 75, 77, 78, 79 (left), 80, 85, 89 (left), 90, 94 (right), 98, 120
Colour Library International: pages 6, 31, 57, 62 (top)
Irene E. Hubbell: page 11
Orbis Polish Travel Bureau: pages 12, 22, 23, 28, 45, 58 (top), 59 (bottom), 64, 66 (bottom), 70, 87, 88, 95
Chandler Forman: pages 47, 48, 50, 56, 61, 66 (top), 69, 79 (right), 84 (right), 93, 94 (left), 121
Wide World Photos: pages 49, 53
C. Barrington: pages 76, 82, 84 (left), 97
Historical Pictures Services: pages 102, 105
Flag on back cover courtesy **Flag Research Center, Winchester, Massachusetts 01890**
Cover: Farms and village in the Tatra Mountains

TABLE OF CONTENTS

The beautiful Tatra mountain range is found in the southern part of Poland.

Chapter 1

A NEST OF EAGLES

LAND OF LEGENDS

Once long ago three brothers lived together in a northern land. Their names were Lech, Czech, and Rus (pronounced "Leh," "Cheh," and "Roos"). The brothers loved their home. Its land was rich and green, watered by a great silver river. Huge trees stood like sentinels all around. From their branches bright birds sang.

But after a while the brothers found themselves with a problem. Each of them had prospered so much in their green homeland that there no longer was room enough for all of them to live there. So one day they went for a walk and Lech climbed a huge tree to see what he could see.

He looked to the south and saw tall stern mountains, lush flat plains, gleaming lakes and rivers, and warm gentle sunlight. He called down to his brothers and told them what he had seen.

"Fine!" said his brother Czech. "I will go to that land and make it my home." And he did.

Next Lech looked to the east. There he saw endless miles of land, vast prairies clothed in golden grass, and broad river valleys filled with animals and birds. He told his brother Rus.

"Fine!" said Rus. "I will go to that land and make it my home."
And he did.

Then Lech looked to the north. There all he saw was the sea. He looked to the west. There he saw thick dark forests filled with strange savage tribes.

"I cannot make my home in either of those places," he thought. "What shall I do?"

Then Lech stopped looking so far away. Instead he looked at the tree in which he sat. And there, right beside him, was a nest, an eagle's nest, and in it were three young white eagles.

"Of course!" said Lech. "Now I know what I must do. I must stay here in this good green northern land and make it my home."

Lech built a town and called it Gniezno, which means "nest." It became the first town in Poland and from that day on a white eagle has been part of Poland's national coat of arms.

That is a legend, the legend of how the nation of Poland began. In some ways, it is true. But it is only one of many, many legends that have been told for centuries in Poland.

Poland is a land of people who believe in things they cannot see as well as in things they can. Perhaps this is because so many impossible things have happened to them in the thousand years of their written history. They have accomplished impossible tasks and won impossible victories. They have lived through times and trials when it seemed certain they all would die.

Another legend concerns a fourteenth-century monastery called Jasna Gora ("Bright Mountain"). It is in Częstochowa, a city in southern Poland. In this monastery hangs a very old picture of the Virgin Mary and the baby Jesus. According to the legend, it was painted by St. Luke. It is known as the Black Madonna, or Our Lady of Częstochowa.

The courtyard of the monastery of Jasna Gora

One day an invader tried to steal the painting. But as he ran from the monastery, he felt the picture grow heavier and heavier. Finally he could no longer carry it. So he whipped out his knife, made two slashes in Mary's face, and left the painting behind. The slashes still can be seen today.

But that isn't the end of the story of the Black Madonna. In 1655, Poland was invaded again, this time by the Swedes. Two hundred thirty Poles had stationed themselves in the monastery, the only fortification left for the defense of their country. Outside swarmed four thousand Swedes. The odds were hopelessly against the Poles, but they believed their Madonna would give them victory—and she did.

The Black Madonna

Most Polish people are Roman Catholics and Mary has always been an important part of their religion. She is even called the Queen of Poland. But the Black Madonna of Jasna Gora holds a special place in the hearts of Polish people. They cover her painted dress with rich hangings of gold, silver, and gems. Each August over a million people travel to Częstochowa to honor her.

Even farther south than Częstochowa lies Kraków, a fairy tale sort of city complete with narrow twisting streets, gingerbread houses, and a castle on a hill. Centuries ago, magicians and alchemists lived on a street called Golembia. They spent their lives trying to turn iron and other metals into gold.

According to one legend, a Polish magician named Twardowski (sometimes called the "Polish Faust") lived on Golembia Street. He made a bargain with the devil. He sold his soul to the devil in exchange for magic powers. When the time came to hand his soul over to the devil, Twardowski outsmarted him. He repented and

Wawel Cathedral in Krakow

the Blessed Virgin came to his aid. He was able to escape the devil, but was forced to spend eternity on the moon—halfway between Heaven and Hell.

Another legend says Kraków was founded by the mythical ruler Krak. The dragon of Wawel Hill had terrorized the people. He demanded that offerings of sheep and cattle be brought to his cave in exchange for the lives of the townspeople. Krak killed the dragon of Wawel Hill.

LAND OF SURPRISES

Visitors to Poland today sometimes feel as if they're walking into a legend. That's because of all the strange and sometimes beautiful surprises in Poland's cities and countryside.

11

*The Mazurian Lakes
are very popular
vacation spots.*

At Oliwa, a suburb of the great port city of Gdańsk, stands a cathedral built in the thirteenth to fifteenth centuries. In the cathedral is an organ with almost eight thousand pipes—and a surprise. When the organist operates a special mechanism, wooden angels ring bells and blow trumpets. And to the sound of triumphant music, a wooden star climbs a wooden sky and announces the birth of the Christ Child.

Not far from Gdańsk lie hundreds of giant blue sapphires. No, they're not real sapphires. They're the Mazurian Lakes, but from the air they look like blue gems nestled in the dark green velvet of thousand-year-old forests. They're full of surprises too, such as floating islands and silent majestic swans, not to mention millions of hungry mosquitoes!

In the far south of Poland tower the giant Tatra Mountains, part of the Carpathian chain. Here still more surprises wait for visitors. Real mountain chalets pop up here and there like life-size cuckoo clocks. Sleighs full of laughing people skim over spun-sugar winter snow. By the light of crackling bonfires people in colorful costumes perform the ancient Robbers Dance.

A mountain chalet in Zakopané

The Tatras are the home of the Gorale people, who still speak their own language and who wear white wool suits with tight-fitting trousers. These are brave people who say they've never given in to Poland's enemies, even when the rest of the country has been occupied. In the mountains, the sad wail of the kobza, a musical instrument similar to the Scottish bagpipe, would sound while the people of the mountains fought on, to the death, if needs be.

When a mountain man does die, his family dresses him in his best clothes, including the white suit, an embroidered coat and vest, and a round hat lined with shells. On top of his coffin is placed the object most important to him when he was alive, his mountain axe, or ciupaga ("chew-PAH-gah").

13

A salt sculpture inside the salt mine in Wieliczka

Beneath the little town of Wieliczka, about 8 miles (13 kilometers) from Kraków, stretches one of Poland's most astounding surprises. It's a salt mine, one of the biggest and oldest salt mines still being worked in Europe. Every day 700 tons (635 metric tons) of pure salt are hauled from this mine.

Deep in the mine are twenty chambers, worked out now and open to the public. These chambers have been declared a historical monument of worldwide importance by UNESCO—and with good reason. One, which is 180 feet (55 meters) long, is called the Chapel of St. Kinga. Statues sculptured from salt stand everywhere, pictures have been carved all over the glistening walls, and from the ceiling hang salt crystal chandeliers, shedding sparkling light on everything below.

Beneath the chapel lie two more chambers and from them a chain of small lakes leads to the Staszic Chamber, which is 137 feet (42 meters) high. During World War II, the Germans manufactured aircraft parts in this chamber. Then there is the Warsaw Chamber, complete with stage, bar, and sports facilities for the miners.

Finally, at the very deepest level, lies a chamber with a museum of the history of salt mining in Poland. Salt mining actually began in Wieliczka in the thirteenth century. Some of the original tools and documents have been preserved in the museum.

The museum's lecture hall is also in the underground chamber, as are a library and a coffee bar.

And there is yet another surprise beneath the earth. In 1964 the Poles built a sanitorium for people with respiratory diseases at Wieliczka. It's 735 feet (224 meters) underground.

LAND OF HARD WORK

There's no doubt about it, people in Poland work hard. Some get only one Sunday off a month, although most get every Sunday off and at least one Saturday, too. The workers aren't all men. Many women in Poland work. Some are doctors and some are street sweepers. Some teach school and some direct traffic. Some operate cranes or pound typewriters or make fine precision tools or machine parts. Most also take care of all the housework and cooking at home.

Polish men approve of their wives taking jobs outside the home. They're grateful for the extra income the women earn. And they're very careful to treat women with courtesy. There is still a lot of hand kissing in Poland.

The courtyard of the Jagiellonian University, Poland's first university, founded in 1364 in Kraków

Children in Poland work, too—and not only at school. Outside some apartments the lawn has been divided into small plots, each with a name, such as Teddy Bears or Bisons. These are the names of groups of children who live with their families in the apartments. Their job is to keep their plot of land clean and well tended.

Poland has many universities and other institutions of higher learning whose students work as hard as everyone else. They realize that their country is going through some important changes. It is changing from an agricultural country to an industrial country—and yet it still has to find ways to get enough

Students enjoy the weather in Market Square in Kraków.

food for everyone. It is a country with a rich cultural heritage, but it needs new voices in the arts, too, voices that will speak for the Poland of today. The students know that the country's future lies in their hands. They want to prepare themselves well to make that future a time of peace and prosperity.

But, of course, no one can work all the time. So there are special student holidays, such as the two-and-a-half-day carnival known as Juvenalia. This takes place every spring in Kraków and gives students a chance to unwind before final exams. They dress up in costumes and wander or dance through the streets. On one corner you'll see Cleopatra, while across the street walks Zorro, with Batman right behind him. A girl has painted bright designs all over her jeans and shirt and her body, too. A skeleton in a top hat is followed by a swarthy pirate.

Adults—including the police—pretty well turn the town over to the students during Juvenalia. The whistles, horns, bells, and funny songs about politicians don't seem to bother them. Maybe they remember their own student days. Maybe they want these students to know that they trust them, not only with their city, but with the future of Poland.

Most of Poland lies on a flat, fertile plain.

Chapter 2

A GREEN
AND OPEN LAND

THE HISTORY MAKER

People are the chief makers of history. But sometimes they have a powerful partner in their history making—geography. This has been especially true for the people of Poland.

Poland lies almost in the center of Europe. It's shaped a little like a slice of bread with the lower left corner chewed away. It covers 120,725 square miles (312,678 square kilometers), which is about the size of the British Isles or New Mexico. Poland is the largest country in central and eastern Europe, except for Russia.

To the north of Poland lies the Baltic Sea and across the Baltic lies Sweden. To the south stretches Czechoslovakia, separated from Poland by the tall Carpathian Mountains. To the west is East Germany and to the east is Russia. There are no natural boundaries between the latter two countries and Poland, and this geographical fact has had much to do with Poland's history.

Most of Poland lies on a flat, fertile plain. That plain often has looked very tempting to Poland's eastern and western neighbors in the past. With nothing but the Polish people to stop them, they've thundered across the borders more than once. As a result, Poland's history has been crueler and bloodier than that of many other countries. The Polish people have had to defend their homeland in one war after another. This made them brave and determined to survive.

SAND AND SEA GULLS

The northern part of Poland is known as the coastal (or maritime) lowlands. Here the land rises gradually from the Baltic Sea to form miles of beaches and sand dunes. In two places the narrow strip of coast dips inward, forming natural harbors. Around one of these harbors sprawls the port city of Szczecin and around the other has grown a metropolitan complex known as the Tri-City, which includes Gdynia, Gdańsk, and Sopot.

The entire coastline stretches for 277 miles (446 kilometers) and is dotted with seaside resorts where people—both Poles and foreign tourists—enjoy sun, sea, and soft sand. Fishing boats bob on the water and sea gulls scream overhead. One strip of the coast has become so popular with vacationers that it is called the Polish Riviera.

In many areas, tall pine forests march right up to the edge of the beaches. Sunbathers who want to cool off can wander along forest paths and buy strawberries, blueberries, or raspberries with cream at refreshment stands.

A part of the shoreline that runs from Gdańsk for about 35 miles (56 kilometers) toward the east is known as the Amber Coast. Fine examples of fossil resin have been found here. Visitors can explore from the seats of a brightly painted little train pulled by a steam engine.

Forests and lakes spread across the northern part of Poland.

LAND OF LAKES

South of the coastal lowlands spreads Poland's great blue belt of lakes. From the Pomeranian and Wielkopolska districts in the west to the Mazurian district near Gdańsk and the Suwałki region farther east, 7,703 lakes are sprinkled across the wooded landscape. Most of these lakes were formed by glaciers in ancient times.

Most of the lakes are small, but some are as large as 40 square miles (104 square kilometers). Many are connected by rivers, streams, and canals to form long chains. There is little industry in this part of Poland. That makes it a perfect place for vacationers who like to relax on sailboat, canoe, yacht, or iceboat. But the woodlands and lakes are also a perfect place for wildlife. There are many specially protected areas for birds and animals. In the Suwalki region live many beavers and in the Mazurian district there is a sanctuary for swans and an island for cormorants.

European bison roam in the Biełowieża Forest.

In the northeast alone there are ninety nature reserves where, among other animals, a wild herd of European bison roams and the largest herd of elk in Europe makes its home. In the forests live wild tarpan ponies, the smallest forest ponies in the world, as well as lynx, foxes, and roe deer.

Birds also thrive in this beautiful area of water and trees. Besides swans and cormorants, there are wild geese, ducks, gray herons, wood grouse, black grouse, and eagles. Eel, pike, trout, salmon, miller's thumb, European whitefish, and crayfish swim in the unpolluted waters.

THE BIG GREEN CARPET

Across the central part of Poland, from the far west to the far east, lies that flat green plain that has done so much to influence Poland's history. Most of the country's farming is done here, although the soil is not always as good as the farmers might wish.

Zakopané in the south is where most vacationers gather to enjoy nature walks, sports, and the exquisite folk art of the mountain people.

Still, the farmers of central Poland manage to supply the country with more food than any other area of the nation can produce.

Most Polish people live in the central plains area. Here rise the big cities of Warsaw, Poznań, Wrocław, Białystok, and Łódź.

THE HIGH COUNTRY

South of Poland's central plains, gentle hills roll into low mountains and plateaus. Many people live in this part of the country because of the good farmland and rich mineral resources. Nowa Huta near Kraków, with its iron and steel industries, is one of the main manufacturing areas. But Katowice, in Silesia, boasts one of the largest coal fields in the world. Mining and metal processing make it Poland's industrial capital.

The far southwestern border of Poland is guarded by the Sudeten Mountains. Their peaks rise less than 5,000 feet (1,524 meters) above sea level, which isn't high as mountains go. But they're covered with forests and drop into gentle valleys and foothills that are good for growing crops and raising livestock.

The Carpathian Mountain system in the southeastern part of Poland stretches up as high as 8,199 feet (2,499 meters), the

Coal mine in Katowice

highest point in the country. Life in the Tatras is quite different from anywhere else in Poland. Time seems to have moved more slowly here.

The wild, beautiful area has slopes ideal for hikers and skiers. The alert vacationer may catch sight of a bear or a chamois (a goatlike antelope) moving through the forests and peaks.

THE SILVER ROADS

Deep in the Carpathians are born Poland's two most important rivers, the Vistula and the Oder. Both flow across the central plains, splitting up into tributaries and streams as they go, until they empty into the Baltic Sea. The Vistula's course takes it right up the middle of the country, while the Oder travels along the western edge. The Bug, a tributary of the Vistula, is another important Polish river and so is the Warta, a tributary of the Oder.

GIFTS OF NATURE

The most generous gift Nature has given Poland is coal. The huge field around Katowice is extremely important to the Polish

Farmers harvesting potatoes

economy. But lesser mineral gifts also lie under the ground, including copper, lead, salt, sulfur, zinc, natural gas, and petroleum.

Nature hasn't been quite so kind when it comes to farmland. Poland has just a little bit of land that is extremely good for growing things without heavy fertilization. This is another important fact when it comes to Poland's history. Her farmers have worked hard. In the past they have raised enough food for Poland and even for some exports. Until World War II, Poland was basically an agricultural country. But in recent years, the government has planned badly. It is difficult for farmers to get tools. Crops are poor and so is the whole economy.

Trees, which cover almost one fourth of the land in Poland, include fir, pine, beech, birch, and oak. In some areas orchards of cherry and apple trees are grown.

Animals also flourish, both in the forests and in areas where more people live. The forest animals include fallow deer, roe deer,

"Juhasi" mountaineer shepherds leading their sheep to pasture

elk, wild boars, lynx, wolves, foxes, badgers, beavers, and squirrels—plus those special animals living in conservation areas. Dogs, horses, cows, pigs, sheep, chickens, and geese help farmers make a living.

Wood grouse, blackcock, woodcock, pheasant, and partridge try to dodge hunters in the woods. Larks greet the dawn and magpies stalk around as if they own the country. Polish waters provide homes for forty-seven different kinds of fish.

A LITTLE BIT OF EVERYTHING

What's the weather like in Poland? Well, that depends on where you are—and when. Usually the coastlands are warmer than inland sections, although some very powerful winds can whip the sand around. The mountains tend to be cooler than lower areas, but sometimes warm air currents come as a welcome winter surprise in the Carpathians.

Many people feel that autumn is the best time to visit Poland. Spring, they say, is too windy and winter is too cold. But autumn lasts for a long, long time and most of its days are sunny.

Chapter 3

FROM TRIBE
TO TRAGEDY

THE SEEDS OF A LEGEND

The history of Poland goes back thousands of years. In the western part of central Poland there is a partially rebuilt Stone Age village. Archaeologists have been busy digging up Poland's early history. But some of that history doesn't lie underground. It lies in the legends and tales that grandparents have told their grandchildren for century after century. Stories such as that of Lech, Czech, and Rus hold the seeds of important historical happenings in such interesting, colorful ways that people have not forgotten them.

Back in the days when Roman legions patrolled the countries of western Europe, Slavic tribes lived in the forests of what are now Poland and western Russia. At first there were few of them and they all spoke the same basic language.

But when the Slavic tribes began growing in number, they decided to spread out. Some went south, over the Carpathian Mountains, to what is now Czechoslovakia. Some went even farther south, across the Danube River into the Balkan countries and Greece. Meanwhile, another group traveled east. They went as

A reconstructed Proto-Dnieper Slavonic settlement used about 2,000 years ago

far as the Volga River in what is now Russia. A third group stayed closer to home, in what are now Poland and East Germany.

As many years went by, different things happened to each of these three groups and their descendants. Each lived through events that formed its own history, different from the other two, but with the same roots. Each developed its own customs and ways of doing things. Each spoke its own language.

Two groups from the same family of Slavic people set out to find homelands in two different directions and a third group stayed at home. That is the earliest history of Poland and the seeds of the legend of Lech, Czech, and Rus.

PEOPLE OF THE FIELDS

The Slavic people who stayed behind in what is now Poland were divided into a number of different tribes. One of the largest tribes was the Polanie. Their name came from a word that means "people who live in the fields." Eventually they gave that name to their country — Poland, or as the Poles call it, *Polska*.

The Polanie were divided into smaller tribes. These tribes really did "live in the fields" on a large plain surrounded by valleys. The valleys were good protection in those early days from neighbors who might want to invade Polanie territory. The soil of the plain contained a lot of clay but the Polanie managed to grow crops anyway. The waterways were far from perfect for transportation, but the Polanie managed to use them as trade routes. They were a tough people, determined to survive and prosper.

At first the Polanie tribes lived in small communities that moved from place to place on the plain. Gradually, though, they began to build more permanent places. These were small towns surrounded by wooden walls and palisades (fences made of pointed sticks) for protection. They were called *grody* and in them the chiefs or princes of the tribes usually made their homes. One of the most important of the *grody* was Gniezno, "The Nest," that Lech named in the legend. Another was Ostrow Tumski, forerunner of the present-day city of Poznań.

Besides the Polanie, there were many other tribes in early Poland. On the coast of the Baltic Sea lived the Kashubs and the Pomeranians. They saw very little of the Polanie, so their language and customs grew in slightly different directions. Those differences remain today.

In the northeastern area of the Baltic coast lived tribes that became the ancestors of the Lithuanian and Latvian peoples.

Slavic tribes lived in the far western part of early Poland. Their land stretched into what is now East Germany. The names of such German cities as Berlin, Brandenburg, and Leipzig come from old Slavic words. These tribes did the Polanie a great favor, although they probably didn't know it at the time. Because they lived so much closer to the Germans, they were the people the Germans usually attacked. This left the Polanie free to live and develop in peace. But it wasn't much of a life for the western tribes. Finally the Germans took over their land completely and made them into Germans, too.

THE FIRST RULERS

To become leader of a tribe, you first must convince the other people in the tribe that you should rule them. Then you have to keep a sharp eye out for rivals who might take your job away. If you want even more power, you have to extend your rule to other tribes, sometimes peacefully, but more often in battle.

As years went by, one family of the Polanie obtained more and more power for itself. The legendary founder of this family was called Piast, but the only fact known about him is that the family took his name. Not much is known about his son, Ziemowit, his grandson, Leszko, or his great-grandson, Ziemomysl, either, except that it took a great deal of blood and violence for them to become rulers.

Mieszko I, great-great-grandson of Piast, is considered the first historic prince of Poland. Early historians first noticed him in 963 when he lost a battle with some other Slavic tribes. Mieszko didn't make losing battles a habit, though. The Piast family had already united many Slavic tribes into a nation and Mieszko went on with the job. At last Poland was recognized by other countries as a country herself. She wasn't exactly a first-class country yet, because Mieszko had to pay tribute to her powerful neighbor, Germany.

Catholics take part in a religious festival.

One of the most important things Mieszko I did was to accept Christianity for Poland in 966. The Roman Catholic church was tremendously strong in those days and Mieszko knew his country needed protection from the Holy Roman Empire. So he asked that the state of Poland be placed under the pope's authority.

But the Catholic church did more than just put a seal of approval on Mieszko's reign and grant protection to Poland. It also sent missionaries to Poland, people who helped set up a government and introduced the knowledge and culture of western Europe to the Poles. Until this time, most of the Slavic tribes had worshiped pagan nature gods. Soon this type of worship vanished or was downgraded to nothing more than folk magic. The Roman Catholic church became a new force that held Poland together as a nation. Over the centuries that force would be tested again and again, but it never failed.

*King Bolesław the Brave
ruled Poland
from 992 to 1025.*

Mieszko died in 992 and his son, Bolesław the Brave, became prince of Poland. Bolesław was a strong ruler who brought more tribes and areas into the nation and reunited the country. He also made friends with the German emperor, Otto III, and ended the paying of tributes to Germany.

But many Germans didn't like Otto's friendship with Poland. Shortly after he died, they declared war. That war went on for many years. Poland was a much stronger enemy than Germany had expected. Finally Bolesław was able to have himself crowned king of Poland. Poland was finally an independent nation.

Unfortunately, Bolesław's descendants weren't as strong as he had been. After he died in 1025, the sons of Bolesław began fighting over the throne. They felt they should have a share of the

Casimir the Great strengthened the government, improved the economy, and encouraged the arts.

power. By the 1200s, Poland was chopped up into so many little sections, each with its own ruler, that it had a hard time defending itself against foreign invaders. Germans, Czechs, Russians, and Tartars all pounced on the struggling nation and tried to grab portions for themselves. For the first—but not the last—time, it was the Roman Catholic church that kept the Polish nation alive through a time of troubles.

Poland wasn't really organized into one kingdom again until the early 1300s. The men who made this happen were Ladislas the Short and his son Casimir the Great. Casimir sat on the throne from 1333 until 1370 and was the last of the Piast rulers. Besides strengthening the government, he improved the Polish economy and encouraged the arts and culture.

TWO HUNDRED YEARS OF GLORY

Casimir the Great had no children to inherit his throne, so he suggested that after he died, his nephew, King Louis of Hungary, should rule Poland. This would have been a good idea had Louis been a fair man. But he treated his new Polish kingdom as another section of Hungary. He granted special favors to the Polish nobles, no longer obliging them to pay any taxes. But in general, Louis ignored Poland.

The Poles agreed to a revision of the agreement made by Casimir the Great in 1355. They promised that if Louis died without a son, they would accept one of his daughters as his successor.

When Louis died, he had no sons. So according to the agreement, Poland would have a woman king. This was very unusual for that time and that part of the world. Louis's younger daughter, Jadwiga, was to be king. The one thing she had to promise was that she would move to Poland.

Jadwiga was just eleven years old when she left her mother and sister in Hungary and journeyed to Kraków for her coronation. Jadwiga was crowned "king" of Poland—once in the cathedral and once outside the Kraków city hall.

It was all like a fairy tale. But the happy ending was yet to come. Jadwiga was engaged to marry Prince William of Austria. Her marriage to Prince William had been officially celebrated in 1378, when she was five years old. She hoped that soon William would be able to come and rule Poland with her. The Poles, however, did not want an Austrian prince ruling them. They thought they had a better idea.

Jadwiga (left) did finally agree to marry Jagiełło of Lithuania (right).

To the east of Poland lay the land of Lithuania, a country that worshiped pagan gods and gave its Polish neighbors a great deal of trouble. If Jadwiga were to marry Jagiełło, grand duke of Lithuania, the two countries could stop fighting and become friends. Lithuania would accept Christianity and would help Poland defeat the German Teutonic knights who were always invading both countries. It was too good an opportunity to pass up.

Jadwiga disagreed. She loved William and she certainly didn't want to marry Jagiełło, that "hairy barbarian" the minstrels sang about. Somehow William managed to get to Kraków and together

Jagiełło's army defeated the Teutonic knights at the Battle of Grunwald in 1410 (left).
King Sigismund II (right) was the last king of the Jagiellonian dynasty.

the two young people pleaded with the Polish nobles to let them wed and rule together. But the nobles were firm. They wanted Jagiełło.

William tried to take over the castle of Wawel. The Polish high officials soon forced him to return to Vienna.

Jadwiga was finally convinced by the lords and especially by the clergy that her duty was to marry Jagiełło. Poland needed this friendship with Lithuania and this would further the progress of the Christian religion.

Finally Jadwiga gave in. She spent the entire next day praying in the cathedral. There is still a plaque beneath a wooden cross in the cathedral that says, "Here knelt Jadwiga."

So fourteen-year-old Jadwiga was married to Jagiełło uniting

Poland and Lithuania. Soon after Jagiełło, too, was crowned king.

Now Poland and Lithuania were united. Their old enemy, the Teutonic knights, were making raids into Polish territory. In 1410, Jagiełło and his advisers attacked the Teutonic knights at the great Battle of Grunwald.

Jagiełło's army made a direct, unexpected attack. The fighting lasted all day. But finally Jagiełło's forces won and their dangerous enemy was defeated. This battle still is considered one of the most memorable victories in Polish history.

Jagiellonian kings ruled Poland for almost two hundred years. Vast stretches of land, including the Ukraine and other Russian areas, became part of the Polish Commonwealth. Both culture and the economy prospered. Politics, too, were healthier than they had ever been. In 1493 Poland established her first national parliament, and in 1569 Poland and Lithuania united under a single parliament. The people of the two countries enjoyed certain basic rights they had barely dreamed possible earlier.

STRUGGLES FOR SURVIVAL

Even while Poland enjoyed the good years of the Jagiellonian kings, an old problem began to raise its head again. The problem was the nobles, who still paid no taxes and who still wanted more power for themselves. They controlled the parliament and were ready and waiting to seize that power as soon as the right opportunity came along.

The opportunity came when Sigismund II, the last Jagiellonian king, died in 1572, leaving no heirs. From then on it was up to the parliament to elect Poland's rulers. The nobles who ran the parliament were not about to elect anyone strong enough to get in

*John III Sobieski
defeated the Tartars
(Turks) at the Battle
of Vienna in 1683.*

their way. They even forgot how bad things had been under King
Louis of Hungary. So some of the rulers they elected were foreign.

It was bad enough that Poland no longer had any strong
leaders. To make matters even worse, though, she had to fight a
lot of expensive wars that ruined her economy and cost her
precious territory. Thirty years of war began in 1648. The cultural
life of Poland fell into a decline. One of the most persistent wars
was with the Turks, whose Ottoman Empire was a threat to many
European countries during that period. In 1683 Poland won a
bright moment of victory by defeating the Turks at the Battle of
Vienna.

It was only a moment, though, and Poland's fortunes continued
to slide during the 1700s. Finally, in 1772, the terrible period of
the partitions (divisions of land) began. Russia, Prussia, and
Austria all were strong neighbors, watching Poland struggle with
her complicated problems. Deciding to take advantage of the
situation, they moved in and each grabbed some Polish territory.
Prussia got land in the west, Russia got land in the east, and

Polish battle dress worn from the 10th to the mid-17th centuries

Austria took its share from the south. Poland lost a third of her territory and half her population.

But her neighbors weren't finished yet. For a while they bided their time as Poland tried to get back on her feet. She reformed old laws and, in 1791, even adopted a new constitution that made the throne hereditary again. But all these efforts weren't enough to stop her greedy neighbors. In 1793 Prussia took more land in the west and Russia took more in the east.

This made Poland fighting mad. In 1794 she went to battle with both countries. Her military leader was a Pole called Tadeusz Kościuszko, who had fought in the American Revolution some years earlier because he believed so strongly in liberty. The war for his own country's freedom did not go as well. Poland lost and in 1795 Austria, Prussia, and Russia divided the rest of her territory among themselves.

On paper Poland no longer was a country. But in the hearts of her people, Poland was still very much alive.

Chapter 4

FROM DEATH TO LIFE

YEARS OF DARKNESS

"France is the only country that can help us now."

That was what the Poles who fled their devastated homeland thought as they made their way west. There was a strong new leader in France at this time—a man named Napoleon Bonaparte. Perhaps if some Poles fought on his side, he would help them put their country back together again.

Napoleon welcomed the brave Polish soldiers into his army, although he never had much intention of helping them in return. In 1807 he defeated the Prussian and Russian armies at Friedland. Then he captured much of the land Prussia had taken from the Poles, called it the Grand Duchy of Warsaw, and gave it back to Poland. But the Poles really had no power. In 1809 Napoleon beat the Austrians and forced them to return some land to Poland, too.

But a few years later, Napoleon made a very serious mistake. He tried to fight the Russians on their own land. He lost. By 1815, Poland was again split up among Russia, Prussia, and Austria. One chunk was known as the Kingdom of Poland, but the Russians really ruled its government and everyone knew it.

Still the Poles refused to give up. They met secretly and

whispered and plotted and hatched conspiracies. In 1830 those Poles who lived in the so-called Kingdom of Poland staged a rebellion against Russia. They lost. From then on Russia would let them have no part at all in their own government.

Once again Polish leaders fled to France, this time to save their lives. There no longer was a Napoleon to fight for, but the exiles found other types of pro-Polish activities. They spent their time letting the rest of the world know exactly what was happening to Poland. They worked hard at keeping the spirit of the Polish people alive.

One of the exiles was a young composer named Frederic Chopin, who told the world about his country through his music for the piano. In his mazurkas and polonaises (pieces based on Polish dances), he announced that Poland had suffered terribly, but was not dead. Someday she would be free again.

In the 1840s the Poles staged more rebellions, this time against Prussia and Austria. Again they lost. In 1863 they tried another uprising against Russia. The Russians crushed them.

From now on, said the Russians, the official language of the Kingdom of Poland would be Russian. In 1870 Prussia formed the German Empire and decreed that all Poles living in the areas she controlled must speak only German. For some reason, the Austrians were not so harsh. They even let their Polish subjects partially govern themselves in the late 1800s. But the Prussians slowly began to tighten their control.

It didn't work. Poles went on speaking Polish, even if they had to do it secretly. Strict controls were placed on the Catholic clergy. Contact with Rome was limited and there was a reorganization of dioceses. But the Poles held onto their Roman Catholic faith more fiercely than ever. And in their hearts they still sang the words of

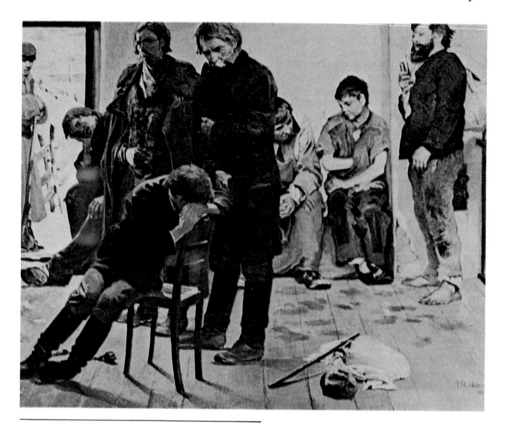

*After the uprising in 1863, Polish exiles wait
to be taken to Siberia in Russia.*

their Polish national anthem: "Poland has not yet perished as
long as we are alive . . . "

A WAR AND A BEGINNING

By the beginning of the twentieth century, signs of new life
were appearing in Poland. Political parties were formed in all
three parts of the divided country and a young leader, Józef
Piłsudski, appeared on the scene. From 1905 to 1907, the Russians
were busy with a revolution at home. The people of the Kingdom
of Poland thought this was a good time to do some rebelling of
their own.

They held strikes and demonstrations and fought a few armed clashes. Even the schoolchildren went on strike. As a result of all this, the Russians said the Kingdom of Poland could organize trade unions, set up cultural associations, and open private schools where students would be taught in Polish.

Then came 1914 and the eruption of World War I. The two giant enemies, Russia and Germany, began to battle one another. And there sat little Poland between them. No matter who won, she would be devoured. Furthermore, the Poles who lived in the Austrian and Prussian sections would be forced to fight against the Poles who lived in the Russian section. It was a no-win situation. But Poland still had to decide which side to support.

"We'll fight against Russia," declared Józef Piłsudski. He had been banished to Siberia for five years and had never forgotten it. So he led his tiny army against the powerful Russian forces.

As commander of the Piłsudski brigade in the Polish Legion of the Austrian army, he soon was known as a national hero. A Polish Army Organization formed by Piłsudski operated in the rear of the Russian armies in Poland. The Russians were driven out of Poland and the Germans moved in.

For a little while, things didn't go too badly. Then, in 1916, the Germans and Austrians announced they had formed a new Kingdom of Poland and would be in charge of its army and foreign policy. Piłsudski and his followers would have nothing to do with this plan. They flatly refused to swear loyalty to the German emperor. So Piłsudski was thrown into a German prison.

As the war dragged on, the Poles liked their German allies less and less. When Germany gave Ukrainia a big piece of Polish land, the Poles had had enough. From then on they worked against the Germans.

At last the war was over. Germany had lost. With help from the Allies, especially President Woodrow Wilson of the United States, an independent Polish republic was formed. As her leader she chose the man who had fought so bravely for her throughout the war—Józef Piłsudski. The Allies saw to it that she got back much of her land from Germany. But getting territory back from Russia was a little more difficult. A war with Russia broke out. The war did not last long and an armistice was signed at Riga on October 12, 1920. Poland did recover some of her lost land.

Now Poland's leaders faced some really tough problems. They had to take three groups of Poles who had lived apart for over a hundred years and make them into a nation again. Furthermore, their economy was in tatters and their government was torn apart by many small rival political parties.

Józef Piłsudski retired from politics in 1923, but soon realized that his country still needed him. There was only one way to help, he thought. So in 1926 he led a military coup, overthrew the government, and declared himself dictator. From then until his death in 1935 he worked at developing Poland's economy, government, transportation, and education. The men who followed him agreed that Piłsudski's way was best and they, too, ruled as virtual dictators.

THE MARCH OF DEATH

But even during the 1930s, while Poland was fighting her way back to recovery, new dangers were growing on two sides. To the east, Russia became more and more powerful. To the west, Adolf Hitler began preparing Germany for yet another war.

"The city of Gdańsk must be given to Germany," Hitler told

Hitler wanted Poland to give him the city of Gdańsk, but the Poles refused. Gdańsk was totally destroyed and reconstructed after the war. Long Market Street looks now as it did before the war.

Poland. "And we want transportation rights in Pomerania." The Poles turned him down.

It was a frightening time. Britain and France had agreed to help Poland if her independence was threatened. But they hadn't helped Czechoslovakia when Hitler gobbled up that country. Russia and Poland had signed a pact that said neither would attack the other. But could Russia be trusted? The United States didn't seem interested in what was going on in Europe. And Hitler had set his sights on conquering all of East Central and Eastern Europe.

Then, on September 1, 1939, Germany invaded Poland. Britain and France declared war on Germany at once, but that didn't help Poland at the time. German soldiers poured into the country. Bombs fell on Warsaw around the clock. The Polish army was no match for such forces, so Polish civilians rushed to the help of their soldiers. In Warsaw, men, women, and children helped put up barricades, destroy bridges, dig trenches, and fire machine guns. Sixty thousand of them died in that battle, but those who survived gritted their teeth and went on fighting.

On September 17 Russia moved in from the east, pounced on the battling Poles, and carried off as many as possible to prison camps. Members of the Polish government escaped to England and thousands of other Poles fled to England and France. There they formed armies of their own and fought side by side with the English and French against Germany.

Meanwhile, the Germans had one plan for captured Poles and the Russians had another. The Germans planned to kill all Polish Jews and make the rest of the Poles virtual slaves. The Russians thought they could weaken Poland by eliminating her most important and best-educated people. Millions of Poles were sent to Russian slave labor camps.

It was a hopeless situation for the Poles, but they were used to hopeless situations. They had faced many of them in the past and had survived as a nation. They would survive this time, too.

The enemy occupation forces were opposed by organized resistance movements. Poles of the underground and partisan units sabotaged the Germans in every way they could.

It didn't take the Germans long to break their agreement with Russia and attack them, too. But still the Russians refused to free all the Polish prisoners.

In Auschwitz over 4,000,000 people were exterminated in gas chambers.
Auschwitz stands as a monument commemorating the martyrdom of those people.

Meanwhile, the Germans were working on their death plan. They found it took too much time to execute people and then bury them. So they began building death camps, places where persons could be brought from all over Europe and killed.

Many of the camps were built in Poland. Three of the most infamous were called Auschwitz, Treblinka, and Majdanek. Those brought to the camps were herded into large chambers in groups of a hundred or more, gassed to death, and then burned in the camp crematoriums.

A warning sign at Auschwitz

In all, Poland lost six million of her citizens during the war. That was 20 percent of her population. Half of these were Jews.

There were many who simply could not believe that human beings would do such things to other human beings. When they realized the truth, it was too late. But other people fought back, including some Jews living in a walled section of Warsaw called the Warsaw Ghetto.

These Jews decided to stage their battle in April of 1943. The only weapons they had were knives, stones, and bricks. But they fought, old people and children and everyone else, and they held out against the Germans for an entire month. When the battle was over, 56,000 of them were dead. Those who'd managed to survive were shot on the spot by the Germans. But somehow five or six escaped to tell one of history's greatest tales of bravery.

Finally, the tide turned against Germany. By August of 1944, the German armies knew their days in Poland were numbered. In Warsaw, the Polish people staged a general uprising throughout the city. They fought the Germans everywhere—even in the sewers under the city.

This is all that remained of the city of Warsaw in 1945.

The Allies begged Russia to help the Polish resistance. But Russia refused. Instead she watched the city of Warsaw bleed and starve. After 90 percent of the buildings were destroyed and two hundred thousand corpses lined the streets, the Russians finally marched into Warsaw. "We have liberated the Poles from their German oppressors," they announced.

The war was over, but Poland lay in ruins. Only the city of Kraków had survived in fairly good shape. That was because the Poles had abandoned it early in the war to keep its beautiful buildings from being destroyed. Thirty million Poles had tried to hold their own against 80 million Germans and over 150 million Russians. Six million died and 500,000 were permanently crippled. Those who survived were stunned. What kind of future did they face?

A monument honors the people of the Warsaw Ghetto. Poles have a custom of placing flowers in remembrance of people and events.

NEW VICTORIES, NEW STRUGGLES

Near the end of World War II, Polish Communists formed a group called the Polish Committee of National Liberation. Its base was in the Polish city of Lublin. After the war, the Russians wanted this committee to become the new government of Poland. The other Allies agreed, but insisted the committee be enlarged to include representatives from the Polish government-in-exile in London and other non-Communists.

Many Poles did not want a Communist government, but the Communist groups used police force to control the elections and get their way. By 1948 they had succeeded. Since then the Polish government has consisted of one legislative house, the Sejm. Its 460 members, elected for four-year terms, run the government and make the laws. Seventeen members of the Sejm are chosen by the other members to serve on the Council of State, which rules when the Sejm is not in session. A Council of Ministers, also chosen by the Sejm, consists of the prime minister, eight deputy prime ministers, and twenty government department heads.

Only about 7 percent of the people in Poland today belong to the Communist party. But members of that party form the majority of the Sejm and both councils. The First Secretary of the Communist party is the most powerful person in Polish government.

In 1948 the Russian Communists gained more power over the Polish government. They managed to get a Russian, Konstantin Rokossovsky, named as Poland's minister of defense. The leader of the Polish Communist party, Władysław Gomułka, wasn't friendly enough to Russia, so he was deposed and later imprisoned.

In 1952 Poland agreed to a constitution that was very much like Russia's. Private people no longer could own businesses. All business was owned by the state. Farmers had to give up their lands and work on state farms. The head of the Roman Catholic church in Poland, Stefan Cardinal Wyszyński, was put in prison.

These new policies didn't last long. The Poles rebelled in 1956, this time with riots. By the time they were over, Gomułka was out of jail and head of the Polish Communist party again, farmers were back on their own lands, Cardinal Wyszyński was free, and the Russian defense minister was sent home.

Meanwhile, rebellions continued. During the 1960s, there were battles between Polish intellectuals, who wanted more freedom, and the Communist government. The Catholic church, too, kept running into trouble with the government. In 1970, many Poles who wanted a better life, a better economy, and better government took part in strikes and riots, especially in Gdańsk. Gomułka resigned as head of the Polish Communist party and Edward Gierek took his place.

Poland borrowed money from foreign countries and began building up industry. But along came a world financial crisis and Poland didn't have enough money to pay back the loans, much less improve living conditions at home. By the early 1980s, many Poles had to spend hours and hours standing in line just to get enough food to keep their families alive.

Once again strikes broke out. Workers demanded political reforms including free labor unions. These strikes led to a consolidated trade movement, called Solidarity. Lech Walesa, the leader of Solidarity, asked for social and economic reforms. Demonstrations in support of Solidarity occurred throughout Poland. Russian troops were stationed near the Polish border and Edward Gierek was deposed from his position as first secretary of the Polish Communist party.

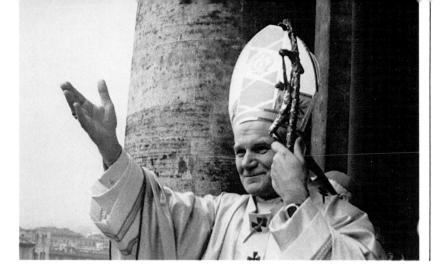

Pope John Paul II

General Wojciech Jaruzelski became premier of Poland in 1981. A power struggle continued between the government and Solidarity. The Catholic church strongly supported Solidarity. Strikes and protests went on and on.

In December of 1981 Jaruzelski suspended the trade union movement and imposed martial law. Lech Walesa and other dissidents were rounded up and arrested. The leaders of Solidarity who were free went underground.

In 1982 Lech Walesa was released and labor unions were dissolved.

Tough times for Poland are not over yet and no one knows when they will be. But Poland still holds on to the things that kept her going in the past. In 1978, a Polish cardinal, Karol Cardinal Wojtyla, was chosen pope of the Roman Catholic church and took the name John Paul II. He is the first Pole, the first person from a Communist country, and the first non-Italian since 1523 to be elected to this position. The Poles are very proud of him. For them he is a religious leader, a national hero, and a living symbol that the Polish people are once again a nation with much to offer the rest of the world community.

*The Old Town in Warsaw was rebuilt brick by brick
after World War II following old architectural plans.*

Chapter 5

CITIES OF STONE AND STORY

Warsaw

THE CITY THAT WOULD NOT DIE

Once, very long ago, a fisherman called Warsz stood on the bank of the Vistula River. Suddenly a mermaid rose up from the waters. She told the fisherman that here on the Vistula a great town would be built, a happy, prosperous, beautiful town.

That legend contains the seeds of truth. A great town was built on the banks of the Vistula and it took its name, Warsaw, from the fisherman—or someone—named Warsz. A mermaid became part of that town's coat of arms and still is today.

Warsaw is divided into two parts by the Vistula. On the right bank is the section called Praga (not to be confused with the city of Prague in Czechoslovakia). Before World War II, Praga was a poor section, but now it has many new industries and housing projects. On the left bank of the river is the rest of Warsaw, including the part known as Old Town. The history of Old Town goes back to the Middle Ages. Another section of the city, called New Town, was founded in the fourteenth and fifteenth centuries.

As a matter of fact, almost all of Warsaw is a "new town" today, although parts of it may not look that way. During World War II, 90 percent of its buildings were destroyed and two thirds of its people were killed or taken prisoner. But the survivors were

Horse-drawn cabs and electric buggies are the only traffic allowed in Old Town.

determined that their city must not die. So, as soon as the war was over, they began rebuilding. Many buildings in Warsaw today are as modern as structures anyplace else in the world. But others look just as they must have looked centuries ago. The people of Warsaw felt these buildings were too beautiful and too full of history to be forgotten. So they carefully rebuilt them just as they had been, using old pictures and plans as their guides.

To visit the Old Town section of Warsaw today, you'll have to walk or ride in a horse-drawn cab or an electric buggy. This part of the city is closed to any other kind of traffic. The narrow twisting streets and the pastel-colored houses give a feeling of being in a different century. Here are fortifications that were built around Old Town during the fifteenth and sixteenth centuries. The Cathedral of St. John was rebuilt to look as it did in the fourteenth century.

One place not to miss in Old Town is the marketplace. There

Castle Square

you can sit at a table in an outdoor cafe, enjoy a cool drink, and look around at the tubs of flowers, art displays, and pink, green, and yellow houses with their steep, tiled roofs.

Not far from Old Town is Castle Square and the Royal Castle. The castle was burned down in 1939 and blown up in 1944. But by 1971 it was rebuilt. Polish kings and presidents used to live in the castle, but now it is a museum. In Castle Square stands a tall pillar topped with a statue of King Sigismund. It was he who made Warsaw the capital of Poland. The statue holds a sword. Another legend says that Sigismund lowers this sword whenever war is coming. The entire statue was destroyed during World War II. But it is such an important symbol to the people of Poland that it, too, was rebuilt.

Above: All these buildings in Warsaw have been reconstructed after being destroyed in World War II. Below: A street leading into the old market square

Warsaw also has modern buildings. Above is a shopping area
and traffic circle in the center of the city and below is the new
train station.

Above: Pedestrians and auto traffic on Nowy Swiat Street in Warsaw
Below: Poland's Tomb of the Unknown Soldier

Swans swimming in a pond in Łazienki Park

Beginning at Castle Square is a road known as the Royal Walk. It runs for about two miles (three kilometers) to another palace, the Łazienki Palace, which is set in the grounds of a beautiful park. Along the Royal Walk stand the University of Warsaw, a place where Chopin lived, the Laboratory of Physical Sciences where Madame Curie began her work, Holy Cross Church, the Polish Academy of Sciences, and the Botanical Gardens. In Łazienki Park is a monument to Chopin; under the monument concerts of Chopin's music take place each summer.

The New Town section also has its share of history and historical markers. The Marie Curie Museum is located in the house where the famous scientist was born. There is a simple manhole cover at the intersection of two streets. Black cobblestones lead to this cover and a plaque on a nearby building tells why. The cover and the cobblestones honor the 5,300 people who fought to defend Warsaw and then traveled through the sewers to escape during World War II.

Above: A panoramic view of Warsaw
Below: The Palace of Culture and Science

Another landmark is the Palace of Culture and Science, given to the people of Poland by Joseph Stalin, who ruled Russia during and after World War II. Warsaw folk joke about this thirty-seven-story building. They say it's the best place in Warsaw from which to view the rest of the city. Why? Because when you're in the palace, looking out, you don't have to look at the palace itself!

There's a lot more to look at in Warsaw—galleries and museums, theaters and parks, the Zoological Gardens, and still more palaces.

There's a lot to see in the countryside around Warsaw, too. About 30 miles (48 kilometers) away is Żelazowa Wola, where Chopin was born. On Sundays from September to June, concerts of Chopin's music are performed by the world's leading pianists. And if all those mazurkas and nocturnes put you in a romantic mood, travel on to Arkadia, a landscape park filled with pavilions, temples, and buildings constructed to look like ruins.

If nature interests you, visit Kampinos National Park and see pine forests, marshes, peat bogs, and sand dunes as high as 100 feet (30 meters), all in the same area. You might also catch a glimpse of elk, wild boars, stag, or badgers. Then, 158 miles (254 kilometers) east of Warsaw is the last primeval forest in Central Europe, Biełowieża National Park. It looks like a forest out of a fantasy land with its wild tangle of majestic old trees.

HOME OF THE FIELD DWELLERS

Out in the middle of the huge, flat Polish plains, halfway between Warsaw and Berlin, lies Poznań, one of the oldest cities in Poland. The Polanie built their first fortified settlement on an island in the Warta River and called it Ostrow Tumski. That was

The Orbis-Polonez Hotel in Poznań is a modern hotel in the center of the city.

in the ninth century. In the tenth century, they began work on a cathedral on the island. Ostrow Tumski became the official residence of the Piast kings. After a while, Ostrow Tumski became known as Poznań. Poznań was commercially important during the Middle Ages.

Poznań was also badly damaged during World War II and its people have had to do a lot of rebuilding. The island of Ostrow Tumski is still there, though, and the cathedral again looks as it did in the 1400s. In the Golden Chapel are the ancient tombs of two of Poland's earliest rulers, Mieszko I and Bolesław the Brave.

Even in earliest times, Poznań was an important trade center. Merchants from the east and the west would travel there and meet to exchange goods—and news—every year on St. John's Day (June 24). In 1922 the Poles revived this custom and began holding the International Trade Fair in Poznań. Now merchants from capitalist and communist countries meet each year in Poznań to take a look at what the other side is doing.

There are other things to look at in Poznań. There are parks and churches, fine old houses, carefully rebuilt, a Palm House full of exotic plants, a museum full of musical instruments, and a sixteenth-century town hall. On top of this town hall is a clock; at noon each day the clock doors open and out pop three goats.

The town of Rogalin isn't far from Poznań. In it is a palace with a park whose oak trees are more than one thousand years old. Three of these oaks measure thirty feet (nine meters) around the middle. Their names are—you guessed it!—Lech, Czech, and Rus.

THE YOUNG CITIES

Because so many older people were killed during World War II and because of a baby boom after the war, one half of the thirty-six million people in Poland are young. This is especially noticeable in certain cities where Polish young people gather to attend special schools and universities.

One of these cities is Wrocław, which lies halfway between Poznań and Kraków. Wrocław is another of the old river cities that date back to the tenth century. So many canals and tributaries of the Oder River crisscross here that Wrocław is known as "The City of Bridges." (There are eighty-four bridges in all.) Wrocław was badly damaged in World War II. But many of its old houses have been rebuilt. Two of the oldest are known as Hansel and Gretel. They stand next to each other and a linking arcade makes them look as if they're holding hands.

Many of the young people who flock to Wrocław enroll at the university, known especially for its science courses. Others study drama at the world-famous Jerzy Grotowski Laboratory Theater or the Henryk Tomaszewski Pantomime Theater. Performances

Above: Poles, in folk costume, celebrating May Day in Wrocław.
Below: The 13th-century Church of St. John on the banks of the Vistula River in Toruń

and theater festivals all year round give the students opportunities to try out what they've learned in class.

Another city that draws students like a magnet is Lublin. It lies in eastern Poland in the middle of a tree-covered upland. No fewer than five universities make their home in Lublin. And when students get tired of their books, they can wander through the Old Town part of the city, which is full of old houses and churches, courtyards, and romantic little nooks and crannies.

Toruń, in northern Poland, has never been a city that liked being told what to do. In the thirteenth century the citizens were controlled by the Teutonic Order of Knights, who had been invited to help subdue the unruly Prussians. But by the fifteenth century, Toruń had become an important trade center. It was decided the knights were more trouble than they were worth. So the citizens sent them home and destroyed their castle. "From now on Toruń will be part of Poland," said the citizens.

THE MAGIC CITY

Kraków is a city of the Middle Ages. During World War II, the Poles abandoned it so the Nazis wouldn't destroy its grand old buildings. For the most part this plan worked.

Today along Kraków's streets there are architectural treasures looming up next to historical monuments and museums and churches crammed with masterpieces of art. Over all stands proud Wawel Hill, a giant chunk of limestone on the banks of the Vistula River. At the top of the hill, Wawel Castle and Wawel Cathedral stand guard. There are some modern buildings—motels and factories and offices—in Kraków, too. But Kraków has something much more special to offer.

Many of Poland's kings and patriots are buried in Wawel Cathedral in Kraków.

Archaeologists have dug up proof that thousands of years ago people lived where Kraków now stands. Wawel Hill was the center of that ancient settlement. We know very little about those ancient people, though, except for what legend tells us.

One legend says that a fire-breathing dragon used to live in a cave on Wawel Hill. (His den can still be seen.) This dragon used to swoop down on the city and devour young girls. No one knew what to do about the dragon until Krakus, a young cobbler, came up with an idea. He filled a dead ram with tar and sulfur and tricked the dragon into eating it. This unusual meal made the dragon so thirsty that he rushed down to the Vistula River and drank until he exploded. Krakus then married the prince's daughter and gave the city his name.

The cathedral on top of Wawel Hill was built by King Bolesław the Brave in 1020. It became the burial place of Polish kings, poets, and other national heroes. In the center of the cathedral stands the

The Old Town section of Kraków

*The Church of the Virgin Mary
where the Heynal is
played from the church tower*

silver tomb of St. Stanislaus, Poland's patron saint. And from the
cathedral tower hangs a huge bell, called Sigismund. It was made
from melted down enemy cannon in 1520 and is rung only on
very important occasions. Wawel Cathedral is also where Pope
John Paul II served as archbishop (metropolitan).

Kraków was the capital of Poland from the thirteenth till the
fifteenth century. A lot of royal business took place in Wawel
Castle during those years. Today the castle is a museum.

Down in the city, the Main Market Square is crowded with
cafes, local people, tourists, and pigeons. Sometimes this square is
called "Kraków's drawing room," because it's where everyone
meets. By the square is the Church of the Virgin Mary with its
uneven towers—and legends.

One of the legends says the church was built by two brothers.
When it was finished, the brothers quarreled and one killed the
other. Immediately the murdered brother's tower began to grow
until it rose higher than the other. The knife that the murderer
supposedly used still hangs in the Cloth Hall.

In Market Square in Kraków stands the Cloth Hall, built in the 14th century as a trading center.

Another legend is still acted out today from one of the towers. Many centuries ago, a trumpeter, who was keeping watch from the tower, saw an army of Tartar invaders headed for Kraków. He put his trumpet to his lips and blew a warning to the people below. Before he had a chance to finish, a Tartar archer saw him outlined against the sky and shot him through the throat. The city had been warned, however, and closed its gates in time to keep out the invaders.

Now, every hour on the hour of every day, that same warning, known as the Heynal, is played from the church tower. The music always stops at the same point when that ancient trumpeter was killed. Polish radio also broadcasts the Heynal at noon each day as a symbol of the spirit of the Polish people.

Kraków is also the home of Poland's oldest university, the Jagiellonian University, founded in 1364. Copernicus was a student here. The astronomical tools he used are on display, as is the famous Jagiellonian Globe, which was made in 1510 and is the first globe to show the American continent.

Kraków used to be surrounded by walls and moats for protection. These are gone now and in their place lies a park, known as the Planty, filled with gardens and tree-shaded walks.

An automobile assembly line at a plant in Warsaw

Chapter 6

LIFE IN A CHANGING COUNTRY

BEFORE AND AFTER

World War II changed the lives of millions of people, including the people of Poland. Before the war, Poland was mainly an agricultural country. Sixty percent of her people worked on farms, and farm products were the most important part of her economy.

After World War II, the new Communist leaders insisted that Poland become more industrial. They built factories around many of the major cities and encouraged people to leave their farms to work in them. Today only 33 percent of all Polish people work on farms and 30 percent are employed by industry. That 30 percent has made Poland the second leading nation of Eastern Europe in the production of manufactured goods. (Russia, a much bigger country, is first.)

THE FIGHT FOR FACTORIES

Getting all those factories started in Poland was not easy. It took money and money was scarce after the war. It took people with energy, too. Even though many Polish people had died in the war, those who survived seemed to have a double supply of determination to rebuild their country. So they got to work and today the things they make in their factories do twice as much for the economy as farm products do.

Most of the things made in Poland's factories are capital goods, such as iron and steel, machinery (especially for factories), chemicals, and ships. These are things used in other industries or exported to other countries. But they aren't the things people go out to buy every day. Poland does produce a lot of textiles and food products, but her factories still don't make enough consumer goods, such as clothes, furniture, and cars, to meet her people's needs. This has sometimes led to problems.

In the early 1970s, life began to look a little better for the Polish people. The country had taken some giant steps in recovering from the war, a whole new crop of young people was ready to start working, and industries seemed at last to have their feet on the ground. It looked like a good time to expand. So the Polish government borrowed billions of dollars from foreign countries and poured them into more and more factories.

But the government didn't plan well. Besides, in 1973 the whole world—including Poland—found itself in the middle of an oil crisis. Oil is important when it comes to running factories, so many of Poland's projects had to grind to a halt. By the end of the 1970s, half of all her money was being used to pay back the loans. That left only half to live on and to import the things she couldn't make herself. People all over Poland felt the pinch.

The government owns 90 percent of all industry in Poland. That's part of its Communist system. Only 10 percent of Poland's businesses are owned by private individuals. They are usually smaller businesses, such as shops or restaurants. Sometimes a

A coal miner working in Katowice. Katowice has one of the richest coal fields in the world.

private individual can rent factory premises from the state and be fully in charge of the factory's operations and the money it makes. But that hasn't happened too often yet.

Poland trades most of her goods with other Communist countries. She is a member of COMECON (the Council for Mutual Economic Assistance), which includes Russia and nine other Communist nations. But she also does a good bit of trading with Great Britain, the United States, and West Germany.

GIFTS AND GAPS

Poland might have an easier time if the land held more natural resources. Nature was very generous when it came to coal—and Poland is one of the leading coal-mining countries in the world. She also has some copper, sulfur, lead, salt, and zinc, and smaller amounts of natural gas and petroleum. But she has to import many things, such as cotton and wool, food products, iron ore, and petroleum. Almost 80 percent of her fuel comes from Russia.

Although forests cover one fourth of Poland, she is not yet in a position to make much money from this natural resource.

Waiting in line to buy food

THE FARMERS' BATTLE

Farmers everywhere are used to battling with the weather and with the land itself. Polish farmers are no exception. Although 60 percent of Poland is farmland, much of the soil is poor. Fertilizers to improve the soil cost money, sometimes more money than farmers can afford. And although the weather can be beautiful during some seasons of the year, winters are long and difficult. There are hungry people in Poland asking for food, sometimes more food than farmers can produce.

But these aren't the only battles Polish farmers have had to face. In 1948 the government announced a policy of state ownership of all farms. Farmers were forced to give up their lands and work on

Farmers loading hay onto a wagon

collective farms, managed by the government. They protested and, in the 1950s, most of them got their lands back. Now 85 percent of the farms in Poland are owned by private individuals. The state owns most of the rest of them.

Farms in Poland are small compared with farms in many other parts of the world. The average private farm in Poland is about 12 acres (5 hectares). An average American farm is 440 acres (178 hectares). The farmers do their best considering the small amount of land and the very few pieces of equipment they have. Many farmers still use horses to pull their plows—and to deliver their produce.

Harvesting kohlrabis, sometimes called cabbage turnips

Rye and potatoes are Poland's two most important crops. Poland is the second largest producer in the world of these foods. (Russia is first.) Polish farmers also grow barley, sugar beets, wheat, oats, flax, alfalfa, and clover. Livestock accounts for 40 percent of Poland's agricultural output and hogs are the most important animals raised. In the south sheep and cattle are raised.

Left: Shopping in a hardware store. Right: A mother buying a special treat for her daughter

WHAT'S IT LIKE?

What's it like to be a worker in Poland? Well, if you work for a business, you probably get to work at around eight o'clock in the morning. You work right through lunch and then, at about four or five in the afternoon, have what is called a "tea-time lunch," a fairly good sized meal. Then you might skip dinner altogether. You work on Saturdays, too, until about half-past one in the afternoon—except for one Saturday a month. Polish workers are eager to have more Saturdays off, but the government says the economy isn't ready for that yet.

Homes and grainfields in the south

You get paid in zlotys. The zloty is the basic unit of money in Poland. One zloty can be divided into 100 groszy, but a groszy is such a little bit of money that is rarely seen or heard of anymore.

Besides a paycheck, you get some special benefits as a Polish worker. Inexpensive vacations can be spent at one of the special facilities maintained for workers by the government. Your medical care is absolutely free, as it is for everyone in Poland.

If you live in the city, your home is probably a two- or three-room apartment. In the country, you most likely live in a small house made of brick or wood. You may or may not own a radio or TV. About half of the families in Poland do own these things. You probably don't own a car. Only 2 percent of Polish families do. Maybe you even have to hold two jobs to make ends meet.

You probably grumble a lot about the government and what a rotten job it's doing for you. But you also realize that conditions have improved tremendously since the end of World War II. And, chances are, you wouldn't move to another country even if someone handed you a ticket. You believe in Poland and you want to work as hard as you can to help it grow and prosper.

PLEASE COME!

One way Poland has tried to boost her economy in recent years is by encouraging people from other countries to visit. Tourism is still a new industry for the Poles, but they're excited about it and trying hard to make it work. They've built many new hotels.

Best of all, the Polish people truly welcome their visitors. They're friendly and eager to show their historical and cultural treasures to others. And they have a lot to show!

Chapter 7

PARTICULARLY POLAND

A KALEIDOSCOPE OF SIGHTS AND SOUNDS

It's a beautiful day in early autumn. You're sitting on a white wrought iron chair at a round white table in an open-air cafe in Warsaw. A fringed umbrella shades the table, but all around the golden sunlight drips like warm butter from a cloudless blue sky.

The buildings nearby look almost as if they've risen from the pages of a children's storybook. Some are pink, some pale blue, some the same gold as the sunlight. The windows of one are covered with iron latticework so finely crafted that it might be black lace.

Street musicians are playing some romantic tune just a few feet away. It wouldn't be too surprising if Chopin were to sit down at the next table. Yes, you're really in the Old World now — practically in another century.

But wait a minute. What's that over there? A very big and very modern apartment building. And farther in the distance? A skyscraper. Come to think of it, the people in this Old World setting are dressed in the latest Western styles. And what is everyone drinking? Cokes.

For a moment there you had Poland all figured out. But then it was as if someone had turned a kaleidoscope, changing the pretty

Left: At the end of this street in Gdańsk is the Church of the Blessed
Virgin built between 1435 and 1502. Right: A brigand's church in Obidowa

Old World picture into a modern scene not so different from
London or Los Angeles. That kaleidoscope will turn many more
times before you leave Poland. It will reveal sights and sounds
that are old and new, Eastern and Western. It's part of what makes
Poland such an exciting and surprising country.

Around thirty-six million people live in Poland today and close
to 60 percent of them live in cities or suburbs. But that doesn't
mean there are a great number of big cities in Poland. Warsaw is
the only city with more than a million people.

All of Poland's cities except Kraków were badly damaged
during World War II. When rebuilding, the Polish people rebuilt
many old buildings to look just as they had in earlier centuries.

The Polish language uses the Roman alphabet.

Poland is an eastern European country with Russia to the east and Czechoslovakia to the south. Surely then her architecture looks Eastern, with onion-shaped domes and maybe a minaret or two. Surprise, again! A few buildings do look Eastern, but not much like buildings in Russia. And many look more like old buildings in Italy. Poland imported a lot of culture from the West almost as soon as she became a nation. Western influences have remained strong throughout her history.

What about Poland's language? It certainly sounds strange — and very much like Russian. It *is* like Russian, because both are from the same Slavic branch of languages. But Polish is different from Russian, too. One of those differences makes life a lot easier for visitors. Polish uses the Roman alphabet. Russian, on the other hand, used the Cyrillic alphabet, which is more like Greek. You may not be able to *pronounce* many Polish words, but at least you'll be able to *read* them.

SCHOOLS FOR EVERYONE

Polish people have always felt education was important. Some of their greatest scholars, such as Nicolaus Copernicus and Marie Curie, are also some of their most popular national heroes. Poets and other artists also are considered to be very important people.

Education is free for everyone in Poland—right through the university level. The law requires children in Poland to go to school from the age of seven until the age of fifteen. School is in session from eight in the morning until four in the afternoon five days a week and on Saturday mornings, too. All in all, Polish children are in class 240 days of the year. When they finish elementary school, they may go either to a four-year secondary school or to a vocational school. Those who are graduated from secondary school can then take entrance exams. If they pass, they can go on to one of Poland's ten universities or to a technical institute or some other specialized school, such as a school for music or drama.

TIME OUT

But even the hardworking, education-loving Poles don't spend all their time at work or in school. They like to take time out for recreation and fun just as other people all over the world do.

Many Polish people enjoy camping and hiking. Poland is full of beautiful places for them to do both. Skiing and other winter sports are also popular, especially in the rugged Tatra Mountains. For those who like to sail, swim, or canoe, Poland has plenty of lakes. People like to hunt and fish, too.

Horseback riding is also an ancient tradition with the Poles and

Skiing and other winter sports are popular.

one that was once exclusively for the wealthy. Poland has long been known for breeding horses and has even sold some Arabian horses to the Arabs!

Although not many Polish people own cars, they have other ways to get around in their country. Both railroads and buses are operated by the state and aren't very expensive to ride. Taxis are cheap, too, if you aren't going too far. But taxi rates double after eleven o'clock at night. Poland has its own airline, called LOT, which flies to cities within the country and also to other countries.

Sopot, a spa on the Baltic Sea

But the cheapest way to get around Poland, especially for young people, is to use thumb power. Poland is one of the few places in the world where hitchhiking is not only legal—it's encouraged. Hitchhikers buy a book of coupons (which doesn't cost very much), then give these coupons to the drivers who pick them up. At the end of each year, the drivers enter a contest and those with the most coupons win prizes.

Some Polish people like to take time out for visits to spas. A spa is a cross between a hospital and a resort, where sick people hope to get well and tired people hope to get back their energy. Often spas are built at places where the water is particularly rich in minerals. Visitors drink this water—or bathe in it—as part of their cure. The biggest spa in Poland is Ciechocinek, near the center of the country.

But for the most part, people in Poland spend their spare time with their families, their friends, and their church.

Left: Very good meals can be had in most hotel dining rooms. Right: In summer, raspberries are a special treat.

RYE BREAD AND SAUSAGES

Meals in hotel restaurants in Poland offer a gourmet trip around Europe. Austrian, French, Italian, and Russian dishes all are available, as well as some Polish specialities. But to eat what ordinary Polish people eat, take a trip to a small village or town. There you'll enjoy a meal of beetroot soup, sausages, cabbage, potatoes, sour cream, rye bread, and, to wash it all down, beer.

Soup is very popular in Poland, but don't expect to drink it out of a mug. Often it takes a knife and fork to make way through a bowl of Polish soup. In the soup you might find sauerkraut, potatoes, peas, barley, mushrooms, vegetables, beetroot, or a mixture of any or all of them. You can have sour rye soup, oat soup, beer soup, or onion soup. In the summer, you might try a cold soup made of pureed strawberries, apples, cherries, blueberries, or raspberries thickened with sour cream. Sour cream,

This Polish woman is preparing a typical meal in her kitchen.

dumplings, and noodles are all favorite soup ingredients. Then there's the famous Polish black soup. It's made with duck's blood, bones, giblets, and dry prunes or cherries.

Meat is sometimes hard to find in Polish stores, but fresh vegetables are very popular and so is fish, such as carp, pike, crayfish, cod, and herring. Polish bread is dark and firm. It tastes a little salty and a little sour, but once you get used to it, you can't get enough of it. The Poles like to eat it with cheese.

After finishing a bowl of Polish soup, there's not much room left for dessert. The Poles usually settle for a mixture of stewed fruits. Sometimes, though, they serve fruit dumplings or pancakes with fruit or cheese. But, full as you might be, don't leave Poland without tasting *paczki* ("PAHCH-kee"), jam doughnuts that taste like a little bit of heaven.

A STRONG CORD

"The church and the faith of the Polish people are the groundwork on which they built their nation. During the years of partition, the church, more than anything, kept the fires of patriotism burning. It is to our religion that Poland really owes its survival."

A Polish priest spoke those words to an American visitor before World War II. They are still true today. Poland adopted the Roman Catholic faith in the year 966 and has held tightly to it ever since. That doesn't mean people of other faiths don't live in Poland. There are some Protestants, some Jews, and some members of different Eastern Orthodox churches. But over 90 percent of the people are Roman Catholic. They worship in about 13,300 churches and study at about 18,000 religious instruction centers. Some go on to the Academy of Catholic Theology in Warsaw or the Catholic University of Lublin. One, Karol Cardinal Wojtyla, has become Pope John Paul II, head of the entire Roman Catholic church.

After World War II, Communist leaders in Poland tried to push the church out of the lives of the people. They sent many priests to prison and refused to let the people take part in many religious observances. It was a drastic mistake. The church meant too much to the people of Poland. To some it meant more than life itself. It was the strong cord that bound them together no matter what else might be going on in their lives. In 1956 they rebelled against the government and the government had to back down. The Polish government still doesn't approve of the church, but it has had to admit that it is in Poland and in the hearts of the Polish people to stay.

EAST PLUS WEST

The Roman Catholic church has also influenced the development of cultural life in Poland. It was the church that sent scholars and artists to the infant country as far back as the tenth century. Because of this, Polish culture shows far more Western influence than does the culture of her neighbor, Russia. Italian visitors over the centuries have helped to shape Poland's architecture and art. French visitors have left their mark on education, science, law, and music, and Germans have contributed to music as well as to literature.

But Poland's culture has retained something uniquely Polish. This is partly because of her history. So many terrible things have happened to Poland that for centuries her writers have told stories about the country as a whole instead of stories about individual people—or themselves. The same thing has been true of Polish painters. During the 1800s, for example, Poland was at odds with both Russia and Germany. Jan Matejko, an artist of the time, painted huge scenes of different moments in Polish history. He wanted to help keep the spirit of Poland alive for his people.

In 1924, a Polish writer, Władysław Reymont, won the Nobel Prize in literature for his novel about the Polish people, *The Peasants.* Henryk Sienkiewicz also won the Nobel Prize for his religious novel, *Quo Vadis?* Other famous Polish writers include poets Mikołaj Rej, Jan Kochanowski, and Adam Mickiewicz, and playwright Stanisław Wyspiański. Novelist Joseph Conrad was born in Poland and so was Jerzy Kosinski, who has written powerfully about what happened there in World War II. Uri Shulevitz, a children's author and illustrator, escaped from the Warsaw Ghetto with his parents when he was only four years old.

*Monument to
Frederic Chopin
in Łazienki Park
in Warsaw*

Polish musicians also have been influenced by the history of their country. Although Frederic Chopin fled Poland during the nineteenth century, he couldn't get his homeland out of his heart or his music. Many of his piano pieces take the form of the polonaise, a dance from the royal court in Poland, or the mazurka, which is known as the Polish national dance.

Other famous Polish composers include Stanislaw Moniuszko (who wrote operas about his country), Henryk Wieniawski (a violinist as well as a composer), Karol Szymanowaski, Witold Lutosławski, Krzysztof Penderecki, and Tadeusz Baird. Performers include Ignace Jan Paderewski (who became a leading Polish statesman as well as a world-famous pianist), Wanda Landowska (one of the world's finest harpsichordists), Artur Rubinstein (a pianist who made many recordings as well as concert tours), and Krystian Zimmerman (a young pianist who won the 1975 International Chopin Competition).

Left: A poster announcing the Jazz Jamboree of 1980
Right: A production of the opera Carmen *in Warsaw*

About the same time the Polish government tried to destroy the influence of the church in Poland, it also tried to control the arts. The only good art, it reasoned, was art that promoted the goals of the Communist party. This led to still more protests and again the government had to back down. Today some exciting things are happening in the arts in Poland. Many Polish artists have specialized in the designing of posters and are now recognized world leaders in this field. Polish musicians have turned to jazz as well as classical music; the International Jazz Jamboree Festival is held in Warsaw every October.

Theaters, opera halls, and movie houses are subsidized by the state, which means they have the money to try new and adventurous experiments. Government subsidy also means that tickets are inexpensive and the Polish people can go to plays, operas, and movies fairly often.

A cepelia display of folk art. Polish folk artists also use what they make. They might eat from pottery dishes turned out by father, store their clothes in a chest painted with bright designs by mother, and stir their soup with a wooden spoon carved by Uncle Józef.

MADE BY FOLKS FOR FOLKS

There's one kind of art that both the government and the people agree must be kept alive and well—folk art. Polish people, especially in the countryside and in small villages, are experts at tapestry weaving, wood carving, pottery making, embroidery, and painting on glass. Special shops, called *cepelia*, have been set up to sell genuine folk art to visitors.

Folk music and dance are an important part of Poland's heritage. Song and dance companies are now subsidized by the government. Many festivals and competitions are held each year. One of the biggest is the Tatra Autumn Festival which draws people from all over Poland—and the world—each year.

THOSE SPECIAL TIMES

Polish people throw themselves into holidays, especially religious holidays, with all the enthusiasm of little children. Christmas is one of the biggest feasts. Two or three weeks beforehand, the priest visits each home in his parish and leaves a special Communion wafer with the family. On Christmas Eve, family members sit around a table and the wafer is broken into pieces. Each person eats a piece, prays, and wishes the rest of the family health and happiness. Then everyone tucks into a huge meal. When that's over, the bells are ringing for midnight mass.

On Christmas Day, presents are opened in the morning and everyone stays home with the family all day. The following day is known as visiting day and the streets are crowded with people out calling on friends and relatives.

When Easter nears, the priest again comes to visit, this time to bless the food that will be eaten on Easter Day. Polish people don't cook on Easter, so this food, which is called hallow-fare, must last all day. The day after Easter is known as Wet Monday. Young children run around throwing cold water on one another and older boys try to catch older girls and sprinkle them with perfume.

Other holidays and festivals are more important in some sections of Poland than in others. In some places during the autumn, people still make straw figures and throw them in the river. This is supposed to bring good luck. Some girls still go to dances on the Eve of St. John and believe that the man they dream of that night is the man they will marry. On All Hallows' Eve (October 31), a number of people visit cemeteries, light candles, and place food on the graves of their ancestors.

Weddings are always a time for celebration. In this country wedding,
the wedding party is wearing national costumes.

But everywhere in Poland weddings are the cause for much
rejoicing. Relatives come from all over the country and sometimes
stay a week or more. Even the poorest family will gather enough
food to make the table—and the people around it—groan.
National costumes pop out everywhere like bright flowers and the
music and dancing go on for hour after hour.

Folk dancing

A PATTERN OF POLAND

The kaleidoscope spins and spins. Folk costumes and blue jeans. Italian buildings with Polish legends. Raspberry soup and Coca-Cola. A Communist government and a strong church. People dancing polkas and people playing jazz. You may feel confused for a while, but all of a sudden these many different pieces will fall into place and you'll see the pattern they form, the pattern that is particularly Poland and no place else.

In the history of every nation there are some people who stand out because of the special things they've done. They are the people whose names we remember hundreds of years after they die. They are the people other people write books about. In a sky full of stars, they are the stars that seem to shine the brightest.

There have been many people like this in the history of Poland—Mieszko I, Queen Jadwiga, Frederic Chopin, Józef Piłsudski, and the five whose stories follow. Each is famous for a different reason. All have brightened the history of Poland by the shining of their own lives.

Chapter 8

SOME WHO SHINE

THE SKY WATCHER

Nicolaus Copernicus was born in the city of Toruń in 1473. His father died when Nicolaus was only ten and his Uncle Lucas became his guardian. We don't know many facts about his early years, but Nicolaus probably went to school at the cathedral where his Uncle Lucas was an official.

When Nicolaus was old enough, he went to the Jagiellonian University in Kraków, which was famous all over the world for its fine work in science. Here Nicolaus plunged into the field of science that would remain his first love for the rest of his life— astronomy. In those days the main authority on astronomy was Ptolemy, a Greek who had lived and written more than 1,000 years before. Nicolaus had some questions about Ptolemy's theories and began making astronomical observations of his own while he was still at the university. He couldn't prove anything yet, but he had taken the first step.

Uncle Lucas wanted him to go to Italy and study church law after he finished in Kraków. Nicolaus obeyed, but he continued to study astronomy—and to make his own observations. While he was in Italy, he made his first important discovery: the distance between the earth and the moon is always the same, whether the

Nicolaus Copernicus

moon is full or not. People hadn't known this before because it was not part of Ptolemy's theories.

Then Nicolaus began to study in earnest. His uncle, who had become a bishop, had him appointed canon of the Warmia Cathedral in Frombork, Poland. This meant he didn't have to worry about money anymore. But it didn't mean he had to work at the cathedral all the time. In those days, the church sometimes paid people just to study and make new discoveries. Nicolaus Copernicus was one of those lucky people.

He stayed in Italy for a few more years, received a doctor's degree in church law, and became a medical doctor, too. At the same time he was making more astronomical observations. Ptolemy had believed the earth stood still in the middle of the universe while all the other celestial bodies moved around it. Copernicus suspected that this wasn't the case at all. According to his observations, the earth itself moved. The reason people didn't feel it moving was because they were moving along with it.

Eventually Copernicus moved back to Frombork and settled down near the cathedral. He set up a laboratory in his home and worked at astronomy whenever he could. A lot of other jobs ate away at his time. He was one of the Poles who tried to get the Teutonic knights out of Poland once and for all. He also worked at developing a better system of currency for his country. And his full-time job was as physician and canon. But in spite of all these interruptions, his astronomical studies went on. Now he was positive that the sun, not the earth, was the center of our system and that the earth was just one planet moving around the sun.

Copernicus didn't tell the whole world about his discovery, though. He was afraid people weren't ready to hear it. But word leaked out anyway and soon scientists everywhere knew about Copernicus's exciting new theory, which he explained in a book called *Concerning the Revolutions of the Celestial Spheres.*

Later astronomers, such as Galileo and Johannes Kepler, would prove that Copernicus's theory wasn't entirely right. But it laid the foundation for future work and that is why to this day Nicolaus Copernicus is known as "the Father of Astronomy."

A MAN WHO LIVED FOR LIBERTY

"He is as pure a son of liberty as I have ever known, and of that liberty which is to go to all, and not to the few and rich alone."

That's what Thomas Jefferson said about Tadeusz Kościuszko, one of Poland's greatest national heroes.

Kościuszko was born in the little village of Mereczowszczyzna in 1746. His family was old and of noble blood, but they didn't have much money. Kościuszko grew up in the same way as many other boys of his time. He was taught at home until he was nine

Tadeusz Kościuszko

and then went to a private Catholic school till he was fourteen. By the age of nineteen, he had decided to become a soldier. He went to the Royal Miltary School in Warsaw for three years and then won a scholarship to study in France. His special interests were military engineering and fortifications.

In 1774 Kościuszko went back home to a whole nest of problems. His father had died and his older brother had spent most of the little money the family had left. The girl Kościuszko loved was married to someone else. His country was being divided up by the powers that surrounded it and there didn't seem to be anything anyone could do about it. In 1775 Kościuszko took a barge to Gdańsk, a ship to France, and another ship to America. In August of 1776, he appeared in Philadelphia and told Congress that he wanted to fight in the revolutionary war. Congress made him colonel of engineers and Kościuszko set about the job of winning liberty for the American colonists.

His first big task was to plan the defense of Saratoga for the Army of the North. He did a superb job and, on October 17, 1777, the enemy surrendered. Next Kościuszko was asked to fortify the heights of West Point. This took a long time and the men working under Kościuszko were badly fed, badly clothed, and, needless to say, not very happy. Kościuszko won them over with his kindness and understanding. He saved some money from his tiny allowance and used it to buy food for the English prisoners, who were even worse off than the revolutionary soldiers. And when he wasn't busy with the army, he worked in his little garden. You can still see "Kościuszko's Garden" at West Point.

After he'd finished at West Point, Kościuszko was sent to the Army of the South. He was to survey all operations, find strategic points, obtain food and water supplies, and decide how to move troops and provisions as quickly as possible. Once again he did a brilliant job. When the war was over, Congress made him a brigadier general and granted him several tracts of land.

Kościuszko went back to Poland in 1784. He hoped he could apply some of his successful strategies to the Polish situation. He soon had a chance. Once again Poland was partitioned, this time between Russia and Prussia. Kościuszko began a rebellion in 1794, and he did it in a way that had never before been tried in Poland. In the past, only the nobles had fought for their country. Kościuszko asked the peasants to join in. They rushed to the cause with the only weapons they had—their scythes. They won some victories, but were hopelessly outnumbered. Eventually the rebellion was crushed. Kościuszko, gravely wounded, was taken away to prison in the Peter-Paul Fortress in St. Petersburg, Russia.

Several years later, Tsar Paul of Russia pardoned him and even gave him expensive gifts. But Kościuszko wouldn't accept his freedom until Paul freed some twelve thousand other Poles in Russian prisons. Kościuszko spent most of the rest of his life traveling in Europe. He made one trip back to the United States, where he again met Thomas Jefferson.

Kościuszko's health was no longer good and he probably knew he didn't have many more years to live. But even in his will he didn't forget the principles of liberty for which he had lived and fought. He asked that the land he owned in America be sold and the proceeds used to buy freedom for black people held in slavery—including some of those held by Jefferson himself. No wonder Tadeusz Kościuszko is a hero to people everywhere who believe in freedom and justice for all.

A WOMAN WHO CONQUERED AMERICA

In the city of Kraków, in the middle of the nineteenth century, lived a little girl named Helena Opid. One day she saw her first play. She became so excited that she caught a fever and had to be put to bed for several days. From then on it was certain—Helena would become an actress.

First she married her childhood tutor and went with him to live in the little Polish town of Bochnia. There were many salt mines around the town. It was an accident in one of these mines that got Helena on the stage at last. A play was put on to raise money for the injured miners and she was in it.

From then on she acted regularly in a small company her husband managed and directed. Her married name was Helena Modrzejewska, but she later shortened it to Helena Modjeska. Life was not always easy for Helena during those years. First her little daughter died and then her husband. Her country was divided up among the Prussians, Russians, and Austrians. When she moved to Warsaw and began to act there, she ran into problems with the

Helena Modjeska as Juliet in Shakespeare's Romeo and Juliet. *In the United States Helena played in big theaters in New York and Boston and tiny ones in frontier towns. All the audiences loved her.*

Russian censors, who wanted to control everything performed on the stage.

Finally Helena and her new husband, Count Charles Chlapowski, decided to move to the United States. California would be a good place to live, they thought, although they were a little nervous about the rattlesnakes and jaguars. Still, they could always eat wild game and cactus fruit and maybe even dig for gold. That's how people thought about California in the 1870s.

So they moved to a ranch and were very happy there—until they ran out of money. There was only one thing to do. Helena would have to start acting again. But first she'd have to learn English. She did that in just a few months.

Her American debut took place at the California Theater in San Francisco. The play was called *Adrienne Lecouvreur* and Helena was a tremendous success, in spite of the fact that her veil caught on fire during the performance. Soon she was being asked to act in theaters all over the country.

Finally the time came for her to make a European tour and act in the great theaters there. Once again she traveled to Warsaw, this time as an international star. Her country was still divided by foreign powers, but a group of students didn't let that stop them. They presented her with a huge bouquet, tied in ribbons of the Polish national colors. "Poland is still alive," the bouquet seemed to say, "and she is proud of you."

Near the end of her life, Helena Modjeska retired and went back to California. She died there in 1909. But she still had one more journey to make. "I want to be buried in the city of my birth," she had said and so she was—in the city of Kraków.

FROM STAGE TO STATESMAN

Ignace Jan Paderewski was born in 1860. When he was six years old he began taking piano lessons. At twelve he started studies at the Warsaw Conservatory. At eighteen he became a professor there. The French composer Camille Saint-Saens once said about Paderewski, "He is a genius who happens to play the piano."

Everywhere Paderewski went, people begged to hear him play—and play and play. His first performance in New York was with an orchestra. His audience said he could forget about the orchestra from then on. They wanted to hear him, alone. And they did. Paderewski gave 117 recitals in just ninety days.

But Paderewski did more than play the piano. He composed music, too, music that had its roots in the dances and folk songs of Poland. In this way, he was very much like Frederic Chopin.

During World War I, when Poland lay shattered under Russian attacks and German oppression, Paderewski used his music in a new way. He toured North and South America, and everywhere

Ignace Jan Paderewski

he first made a speech, begging for money for the starving and dying people in Poland. "I come to speak to you of a nation which is not yours," he began, "in a language which is not mine." After his speech, he played the music of Chopin.

By the time the war was over, Poland knew he was one of her greatest statesmen. He represented her at the Versailles peace conference and at the League of Nations. It was largely through his efforts that Poland became an independent nation again. He was chosen to be her premier and her minister of foreign affairs. And he gave her almost all the money he had earned as a pianist.

In 1922 Paderewski began giving concerts again. When he was seventy-eight years old and touring in America, he had a slight heart attack. So he went back to the home he had bought in Switzerland to rest. After just a few months, Germany invaded Poland. World War II had begun and once again Paderewski rushed to help his country. He became president of the Polish parliament in exile and did all he could to serve Poland until his death in 1941.

Marie Curie was not selfish with her discoveries. She shared them with scientists all over the world and she helped found Radium Institutes in Paris and Warsaw.

THE PRACTICAL DREAMER

Maria Skłodowska's grandfather was president of a school in Lublin. Her parents were teachers in Warsaw. It wasn't surprising that Maria loved to learn, or that she was graduated at the head of her class when she was fifteen. But Maria had been born in Warsaw in 1867, a time when the Russians were in control of that part of Poland. That didn't help to make learning easy.

Maria had to work hard to get together enough money to go to school. For a while, she was a governess for a family who lived in the country. In her spare time she studied on her own and also organized classes for the village children. The Russians said these children couldn't have an education. Maria ignored the Russians.

Finally she had enough money to attend the Sorbonne, the famous university in Paris. She had to live in an attic room and was as poor as a street sparrow, but she was happy as a lark, too. She was doing graduate work in physics, chemistry, and mathematics and that was what she'd wanted to do most of all.

After she was graduated, Marie (French for Maria) married a

French scientist, Pierre Curie. Together they discovered two new chemical elements. They named them radium and—for Poland—polonium. They and another man, who was working in the same area of research, received the Nobel Prize in physics in 1903. Pierre died in 1906 and Marie was given his job as a professor at the Sorbonne. She went on working with radium and polonium and received the 1911 Nobel Prize in chemistry.

During World War I, she took a radiographic unit to the battlefront so wounded soldiers could be X-rayed. Her daughter, Irene, went with her as a nurse. Later Marie worked with Irene and Irene's husband, Frederic Joliet, in atomic research. She died in 1934 of leukemia.

Marie Curie's scientific work gave much to the world, but so did her way of thinking about science. "Scientific work must not be considered from the point of view of the direct usefulness of it," she once said. "It must be done for itself, for the beauty of science, and then there is always the chance that a scientific discovery may become like radium a benefit for humanity." She really was a practical dreamer.

THE REAL HEROES

People like Copernicus, Kościuszko, Modjeska, Paderewski, and Curie have done much for Poland and the world. They are real heroes. But so are the nameless people—those who built the first *grody* and planted the first seeds, those who died in Russian slave labor camps or in heroic Warsaw, those who mine coal or pound typewriters or raise children today. They, too, have devoted their lives to their country. Poland will not perish as long as such nameless heroes live.

Cities and towns in Poland

City	Grid	City	Grid	City	Grid
Aleksandrów	B5	Końskie	C6	Przemyśl	D7
Augustów	B7	Kościan	B4	Przeworsk	C7
Biała Podlaska	B7	Kościerzyna	A4	Pszczyna	D5
Białogard	A4	Kostrzyń	B3	Puławy	C6
Białystok	B7	Koszalin	A4	Pułtusk	B6
Bielawa	C4	Kozienice	C6	Racibórz	C5
Bielsko-Biała	D5	Koźle	C5	Radom	C6
Bielsk Podlaski	B7	Kożuchów	C3	Radomsko	C5
Bochnia	D6	Kraków	C5	Rawa Mazowiecka	C6
Brodnica	B5	Kraśnik Lubelski	C7	Rawicz	C4
Brzeg	C4	Krasnystaw	C7	Rembertów (part of Warsaw)	B6
Brzeziny	C5	Krosno	D6	Reszel	A6
Busko	C6	Krosno Odrzańskie	B3	Rogoźno	B4
Bydgoszcz	B5	Krotoszyn	C4	Rybnik	C5
Bystrzyca	C4	Kruszwica	B5	Rypin	B5
Bytom	C5	Krynki	B7	Rzeszów	C6
Chełm	C7	Kutno	B5	Sandomierz	C6
Chełmno	B5	Kwidzyń	B5	Sanok	D7
Chełmża	B5	Łańcut	C7	Siedlce	B7
Chodzież	B4	Lębork	A4	Sieradz	C5
Chojna	B3	Łeczyca	B5	Sierpc	B5
Chojnice	B4	Legnica	C4	Skierniewice	C6
Chojnów	C3	Leszno	C4	Słupca	B4
Ciechanów	B6	Lipno	B5	Słupsk	A4
Cieszyn	D5	Łódź	C5	Sochaczew	B6
Czersk	B4	Łomza	B7	Sokołów	B7
Częstochowa	C5	Łowicz	B5	Sopot	A5
Dab (part of Szczecin)	B3	Lubań	C3	Sosnowiec	C5
Dąbrowa	C6	Lubartów	C7	Starachowice	C6
Dąbrowa Górnicza	C5	Lublin	C7	Stargard	B3
Darłowo	A4	Lubliniec	C5	Starogard	B5
Dębica	C6	Lukow	C7	Strzegom	C4
Dębno	B3	Malbork	A5	Strzelce	C5
Działdowo	B6	Miechów	C6	Strzelin	C4
Dzierżoniów	C4	Miedzyrzec	C7	Strzelno	B5
Elblag	A5	Mielec	C6	Sucha	D5
Elk	B7	Mława	B6	Suwałki	A7
Gąbin	B5	Modlin	B6	Świdnica	C4
Garwolin	C6	Mogilno	B4	Świdwin	B3
Gdańsk	A5	Myślenice	D5	Świebodzice	C4
Gdynia	A5	Nakło	B4	Świebodzin	B3
Gliwice	C5	Nisko	C7	Swiecie	B5
Głubczyce	C4	Nowa Sól	C3	Swinoujście	B3
Głuchołazy	C4	Nowy Sacz	D6	Szamotuły	B4
Gniezno	B4	Nowy Targ	D6	Szczebrzeszyn	C7
Gorlice	D6	Nysa	C4	Szczecin	B3
Gorzów	B3	Okecie (part of Warsaw)	B6	Szczecinek	B4
Gostyń	C4	Oława	C4	Tarnobrzeg	C6
Gostynin	B5	Olesno	C5	Tarnów	C6
Grajewo	B7	Olsztyn	B6	Tczew	A5
Grodzisk	B4	Opatów	C6	Tomaszów Lubelski	C7
Grójec	C6	Opoczno	C6	Tomaszów Mazowiecki	C6
Grudziądz	B5	Opole	C4	Toruń	B5
Hrubieszów	C7	Opole Lubelskie	C6	Tuchola	B4
Inowrocław	B5	Ostróda	B5	Turek	B5
Janów Lubelski	C7	Ostrołeka	B6	Wągrowiec	B4
Jarocin	C4	Ostrowiec	C6	Wałbrzych	C4
Jarosław	C7	Ostrów Mazowiecka	B6	Warsaw	B6
Jawor	C4	Ostrów Wielkopolski	C4	Wejherowo	A5
Jedrzejów	C6	Ostrzeszów	C4	Wieliczka	C6
Jelenia Góra	C3	Oświęcim	C5	Wieluń	C5
Kalisz	C5	Ozorków	C5	Włocławek	B5
Kartuzy	A5	Pabianice	C5	Wrocław	C4
Katowice	C5	Paczków	C4	Ząbkowice	C4
Kępno	C5	Piła	B4	Zabrze	C5
Ketrzyn Mazowiecki	A6	Piotrków	C5	Zakopané	D5
Kęty	D5	Pleszew	C4	Zamość	C7
Kielce	C6	Płock	B5	Zawiercie	C5
Kłobuck	C5	Płońsk	B6	Zduńska Wola	C5
Klodzko	C4	Poznań	B4	Zgierz	C5
Kluczbork	C5	Prudnik	C4	Zielona Góra	C3
Koło	B5	Pruszków	B6	Zyrardów	B6
Konin	B5	Przasnysz	B6		

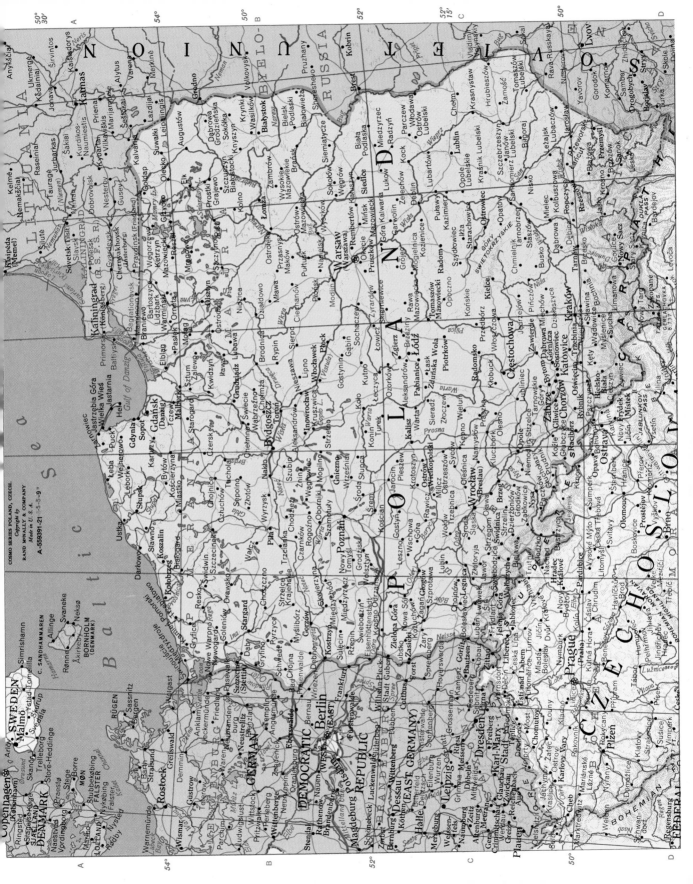

MINI-FACTS AT A GLANCE

GENERAL INFORMATION

Official Name: Polish People's Republic

Capital: Warsaw

Official Language: Polish. The Roman alphabet is used.

National Government: In theory, Poland is a people's republic. But the country is actually controlled by the Polish United Workers party (Communist party). However, only 7 percent of the total population belongs to the Communist party.

There is a one-house legislature called the Sejm. Its 460 members are elected to four-year terms. The Council of State, made up of seventeen members of the Sejm, performs the functions of the Sejm when it is not in session. A Council of Ministers is also appointed by the Sejm. It includes the prime minister, eight deputy prime ministers, and twenty other ministers who head various government departments.

Local Government: Poland is divided into forty-six provinces *(voivodships)*. These provinces are subdivided into counties *(powiat)* and smaller municipal and rural administrative units called *gminas*.

Courts: The Supreme Court is the highest court in Poland. Judges are appointed for five-year terms by the Council of State.

Armed Forces: Men may be drafted at the age of eighteen to serve for a minimum of two years. Poland is a member of the Warsaw Treaty Organization.

Coat of Arms: The coat of arms features a white eagle set against a red shield.

Flag: The eagle used on the coat of arms also appears on the red-and-white state flag. However, the national flag, used by the people, omits the eagle.

National Song: "Poland Has Not Yet Perished," composed in 1797

Religion: More than 94 percent of the people remain loyal to the Roman Catholic church. There are about 13,000 Roman Catholic churches in Poland, even though the Communist party officially discourages religious practices.

Money: The basic unit is the zloty. In 1988, about 400 zlotys equaled $1.00 in United States currency.

Weights and Measures: Metric system

Population: 38,389,000 (1989 estimate). Distribution is approximately 60 percent urban and 40 percent rural. Density is 317 persons per sq. mi. (125 per km^2).

Cities: The largest cities are:

Warsaw	1,600,000
Łódź	848,000
Kraków	740,000
Wrocław	631,000
Poznań	570,000
Gdańsk	no estimate
Szczecin	no estimate

(Population figures based on 1987 official estimates.)

GEOGRAPHY

Borders:
    North—Baltic Sea
    South—Czechoslovakia
    West—German Democratic Republic (East Germany)
    East—Soviet Union (Russia)

Highest Point: Rysy Peak, 8,199 ft. (2,499 m)

Lowest Point: Sea level

Rivers: Rivers and canals form a network of navigable waterways. The longest river is the Vistula, 675 mi. (1,086 km) long. Other major rivers include the Bug, a tributary of the Vistula; the Oder; and the Warta, a tributary of the Oder.

Lakes: There are about 7,700 lakes, most of them in the area south of the coastal lowlands. Many of these lakes were formed by glaciers in earlier times.

Mountains: The Sudeten Mountains are found in southwestern Poland, and the Western Carpathian Mountains form the southernmost region of Poland. The two ranges are separated by a mountain pass called Moravian Gate.

Climate: The coast generally has milder weather than the inland areas, and the mountains are cooler than the lowlands. Temperatures average 26° F. (-3° C.) in January and 73° F. (23° C.) in July. Average annual precipitation totals 24 in. (61 cm).

Greatest Distances: East to west—430 mi. (692 km)
                         North to south—395 mi. (636 km)
                         Coastline: 277 mi. (446 km)

Area: 120,725 sq. mi. (312,677 km²). Poland is the largest country in central and eastern Europe except for the Soviet Union.

NATURE

Soils: Poland has extremely variable soils, with the richest soils being found in the south.

Trees: Fir, pine, beech, birch, oak. Also orchards of cherry and apple trees.

Birds: Wild geese, ducks, gray herons, wood grouse, blue grouse, eagles, blackcock, pheasant, partridges, larks, and magpies. Poland has a sanctuary for swans and an island for cormorants.

Fish: Eel, pike, trout, salmon, miller's thumb, European whitefish, and crayfish are only a few of the forty-seven different types of fish found in Polish waters.

Animals: Wild tarpan ponies, lynx, foxes, roe deer, fallow deer, wild boars, wolves, badgers, beavers, squirrels

EVERYDAY LIFE

Food: Meals often feature a thick soup, *bigos*, which is eaten with fork and knife. Fresh vegetables and fish are also popular. Dessert is generally stewed fruit. In recent years, Poland has been troubled by rising food prices and shortages, especially of products such as fresh meat.

Homes: Most city families live in two- or three-room apartments. Rural families most often have small brick or wooden cottages.

Medical Care: Provided free by the government

Schools: About 98 percent of the Poles can read and write. Education is free and the school system is run by the government through the Ministry of Education and Higher Learning. Children between the ages of seven and fifteen are required to attend school. Students may also attend vocational or four-year secondary schools. Examinations must be passed to be admitted to schools of higher education.

There are ten universities and almost one hundred state universities and other university-level schools. The oldest university, the University of Kraków (now Jagiellonian University), was founded in 1364. There is one private university, the Catholic University of Lublin.

Holidays: Religious holidays, such as Christmas and Easter, are festive celebrations, at which folk costumes still might be worn. Weddings are also important events, especially in the rural areas.

Official public holidays include New Year's Day (January 1); the Monday after Easter; Labor Day (May 1); Corpus Christi (1st Thursday after Trinity Sunday); National Liberation Day (July 22); All Saints' Day (November 1); and Christmas (December 25 and 26).

Special festivals include a two-and-a-half day student carnival known as Juvenalia every spring in Kraków. Students dress in costumes and there is much dancing in the streets. Also there are many folk festivals; the Tatra Autumn festival is one of the largest.

Folk Art: Polish people are experts at tapestry weaving, wood carving, pottery making, embroidery, and painting on glass. Special shops, called *cepelia*, have been set up to sell to visitors..

Recreation: Camping, hiking, skiing and other winter sports, sailing, swimming, canoeing, fishing, and horseback riding are popular.

Communications: About eighty newspapers are published, with a total circulation of about 8.5 million copies. There are also three radio networks and two television stations.

Transportation: Railroads are the chief means of transportation. Cities are linked by about 16,500 mi. (26,550 km) of track. There are also about 190,000 mi. (306,000 km) of roads, but less than half are paved. However, only 2 percent of Poles own automobiles. A single airline, Polish Airlines (LOT), operates both domestic and foreign flights. Seaports include Gdańsk, Gdynia, and Szczecin. Hitchhiking is encouraged.

Occupations: About 30 percent of workers are in agriculture and forestry, 44 percent in manufacturing, and 11 percent in service industries. Tourism is growing in importance. Many women work, especially in the areas of health and social welfare.

Principal Products:
Agriculture: Poland is the world's second largest producer of potatoes and rye. Other leading crops include barley, sugar beets, and wheat. Hogs, cattle, and sheep are also raised.
Industry: Chemicals, food products, iron and steel, machinery, ships, textiles
Mining: Coal, copper, lead, salt, sulfur, zinc, natural gas

IMPORTANT DATES

800s — Slavic tribes unite under the Polanie

966 — Poles adopt Christianity

1025 — Bolesław I crowned first king of Poland, just before his death

1364 — Kraków University founded

1386 — Jagiellonian dynasty founded

1493 — First national parliament

1500s — Polish Commonwealth or Royal Republic reaches height of power

1569—Poland and Lithuania unite under single parliament

1772—First partition of Poland carried out by Austria, Prussia, and Russia

1793—Russia and Prussia carried out second partition of Poland

1795—The third partition of Poland

1918—Poland proclaims itself an independent republic

1939—Poland invaded and partitioned by Germany and Russia

1945—A Communist-dominated government forced upon the people of Poland; Poland's present boundaries established

1952—Constitution similar to Russia's goes into effect

1956—Władysław Gomułka becomes head of the Communist party following antigovernment demonstrations in Posnań and Warsaw

1970—Following strikes and riots, Edward Gierek becomes the new head of the Communist party

1978—Karol Cardinal Wojtyla, archbishop of Kraków, elected pope of the Roman Catholic church; he takes the name of John Paul II

1980—Stanislaw Kania becomes leader of the Communist party following worker strikes demanding political and economic reform; Solidarity, an organization of about fifty trade unions under the leadership of Lech Walesa, is recognized; workers win the right to have free labor unions with right to strike

1981—Wojciech Jaruzelski becomes new head of Communist party; Rural Solidarity, an independent farmers' union, is recognized; in December, the trade union movement is suspended and martial law declared

1982—Continuous power struggles between the Communist government and Solidarity, which is strongly supported by the Catholic church

1983—Archbishop Jozef Glemp named a cardinal by Pope John Paul II

1987—Government announces price increases up to 100 percent on food, gasoline, transportation, and postal services in a severe economic austerity program

1988—Warsaw Pact meeting in Vienna proposes new cutbacks in military strength for each Alliance by 1996

1989—Solidarity leader Tadeusz Mazowiecki, a non-Communist, is elected Prime Minister of Poland

IMPORTANT PEOPLE

Stephen Báthory (1533-1586), one of the greatest rulers of Poland

Frederic F. Chopin (1810-1849), composer, born near Warsaw

Joseph Conrad (1857-1924), novelist, born in Kiev

Nicolaus Copernicus (1473-1543), astronomer, born in Toruń

Maria Sklodowska-Curie (1867-1934), received Nobel Prizes in physics (1903) and chemistry (1911), born in Warsaw

Jozef Cyrankiewicz (1912-1989), Premier 1947-1952 and 1954-1970

Roman Dmowski (1864-1939), politician, in 1917 formed the Polish National Committee in Paris to win Allied support for an independent Poland

Casimir Funk (1884-1967), biochemist, discovered the concept of vitamins, born in Warsaw

Edward Gierek (1913-   ), leader of Polish Communist party from 1970 to 1980, born in Porabka, near Katowice

Mikolaj Gomólka (1535-1609), composer, born in Sandomierz

Wladyslaw Gomulka (1905-   ), head of Communist party from 1956 to 1970, born in Krosno

Jerzy Grotowski (1933-   ), founder of experimental Wrocław Laboratory Theater

Marek Hlaszko (1933-1968), novelist

John III Sobieski (1624-1696), king of Poland, born in Olesko

John Paul II (Karol Cardinal Wojtyla) (1920-   ), first Polish pope in history, first pope from a Communist country, and first non-Italian pope since 1523, born in Wadowice

Jan Kochanowski (1530-1584), poet, one of the first to use the Polish language in his works

Tadeusz Kościuszko (1746-1817), general, led Polish forces against Russia and Prussia, also fought in American Revolution, born in Lithuania

Wanda Landowska (1879-1959), harpsichordist, born in Warsaw

Karol Lipinski (1790-1861), violin virtuoso and composer

Witold Lutoslawski (1913-   ), pianist and composer, born in Warsaw

Bronislaw Malinowski (1884-1942), anthropologist, known for study of the culture of the peoples of Tribriand Islands, born in Kraków

Jan Matejko (1838-1893), painter

Adam Mickiewicz (1798-1855), poet

Czeslaw Milosz (1911-   ), poet, winner of 1980 Nobel Prize in literature

Helena Modjeska (1840-1909), actress, born in Kraków

Stanislaw Moniuszko (1819-1872), composer, born in Ubiel

Karol Olszewski (1846-1915), physicist, with Zygmunt Wroblewski liquefied oxygen and nitrogen

Ignace Jan Paderewski (1860-1941), statesman and pianist, born in Podolia in the Ukraine

Krzysztof Penderecki (1933-   ), composer, born in Dębica

Józef Piłsudski (1867-1935), political figure, led Polish forces on side of Austria against Russia in World War I, became first chief of state, later led military overthrow of government and ruled as dictator, born in Wilno (Vilnois)

Casimir Pulaski (1747-1779), military leader in American Revolution, born in Podolia, now part of the Soviet Union

Mikołaj Rej (1505-1569), writer, one of first to use Polish language in works, called "Father of Polish literature"

Władysław Reymont (1867-1925), novelist, received 1924 Nobel Prize in literature

Ludomir Rozycki (1884-1953), composer, born in Warsaw

Artur Rubinstein (1887-1982), pianist, born in Łódź

Waclaw Sierpinski (1882-1969), mathematician

Henryk Sienkiewicz (1846-1916), novelist, received 1905 Nobel Prize in literature, born in Siedlce, Russian Poland

Juliusz Stowacki (1809-1849), romantic poet and dramatist

Karol Szymanowaski (1882-1937), composer, born in Tymoszouka, Ukraine

Andrzej Wajda (1926-   ), film director, born in Suwałki

Lech Walesa (1943-   ), union organizer, head of Solidarity, born in Popow

Adam Wazyk (1905-   ), poet, author, and translator

Henryk Wieniawski (1835-1880), violinist and composer, born in Lublin

Zygmunt Wroblewski (1845-1888), chemist, with Karol Olszewski liquefied oxygen and nitrogen

Stanisław Wyspiański (1869-1907), painter, poet, and playwright

Stefan Cardinal Wyszyński (1901-1981), head of Roman Catholic church in Poland, born in Zuzela

Stefan Żeromski (1864-1925), novelist and playwright

RULERS OF POLAND

DYNASTY OF PIAST	Reign
Mieszko I	c. 960-992
Bolesław I (Bolesław the Brave)	992-1025
Mieszko II	1025-1034
PERIOD OF ANARCHY	1034-1038
Casimir (Casimir the Restorer)	1038-1058
Bolesław II (Bolesław the Bold)	1058-1079
Ladislaw I Hermann	1079-1102
Bolesław III Wrymouth	1102-1138
Ladislav II	1138-1145

Bolesław IV	1146-1173
Mieszko III (Mieszko the Old)	1173-1177
Casimir II (Casimir the Just)	1177-1194
Leszek I (Leszek the White)	1194-1227
Bolesław V (Bolesław the Chaste)	1227-1279
Leszek the Black	1279-1289
Ladislas I (Lokietek the Short)	1289-1290
Przemyslaw II	1290-1296
Ladislas IV (Lokietek, restored)	1296-1300
Wenceslaus I	1300-1305
Ladislaw IV, Lokietek	1305-1333
Casimir III (Casimir the Great)	1333-1370
Louis of Anjou (king of Poland and Hungary)	1370-1382
Jadwiga and Ladislas Jagiełło (co-kings)	1386-1399

DYNASTY OF JAGIELLONIAN

Ladislas V	1386-1399
Ladislas V Jagiełło	1399-1434
Ladislas VI	1434-1444
Casimir IV	1447-1492
John Albert (John I)	1492-1501
Alexander I	1501-1506
Sigismund I (Sigismund the Old)	1506-1548
Sigismund II (Augustus)	1548-1572

ELECTIVE MONARCHY

Henry of Valois	1573-1574
Stephen Báthory	1575-1586
Sigismund III (Vasa)	1587-1632
Ladislas VII	1632-1648
John II Casimir (Casimir V)	1648-1668
Michael Wiśniowiecki	1669-1673
John III Sobieski	1674-1696
Augustus II (Frederick Augustus I)	1697-1704
Stanislas I Leszczynski	1704-1709
Augustus II, restored	1709-1733
Stanislas I, restored	1733-1734
Augustus III	1734-1763
Stanislas II	1764-1795

PERIOD OF FOREIGN RULE	1793-1908	PEOPLE'S DEMOCRACY	
		Bolesław Bierut	1944-1952
REPUBLIC OF POLAND		Alexander Zawadzki	1952-1964
Józef Piłsudski	1919-1922	Edward Ochab	1964-1968
Gabrjel Narutowicz	1922-1922	Marian Spychalski	1968-1970
Stanislaw Wojciechowski	1922-1926	Józef Cyrankiewicz	1970-1972
Ignace Moscicki	1926-1939	Henryk Jablonski	1972-

LEADERS OF COMMUNIST PARTY

GERMAN OCCUPATION	1939-1945	Władysław Gomułka	1956-1970
Władysław Raczkiewicz	1939-1947	Edward Gierek	1970-1980
(government-in-exile in London)		Stanislaw Kania	1980-1981
		Wojciech Jaruzelski	1981-

INDEX

Page numbers that appear in boldface type indicate illustrations

About the Author

Carol Greene has a B.A. in English Literature from Park College, Park-ville, Missouri and an M.A. in Musicology from Indiana University, Bloom-ington. She's worked with international exchange programs, taught music and writing, and edited children's books. She now works as a free-lance writer in St. Louis, Missouri and has had published over 20 books for children and a few for adults. When she isn't writing, Ms. Greene likes to read, travel, sing, and do volunteer work at her church. Her other books for Childrens Press include: *The Super Snoops and the Missing Sleepers; Sandra Day O'Connor: First Woman on the Supreme Court; Rain! Rain!; Please, Wind?; Snow Joe;* and *The New True Book of Holidays Around the World.*